ROUTLEDGE LIBRARY EDITIONS: HUMAN RESOURCE MANAGEMENT

Volume 5

TELECOMMUTING

TELECOMMUTING
Modeling the Employer's and the Employee's Decision-Making Process

ADRIANA BERNARDINO

Routledge
Taylor & Francis Group

LONDON AND NEW YORK

First published in 1996 by Garland Publishing, Inc.

This edition first published in 2017
by Routledge
2 Park Square, Milton Park, Abingdon, Oxon OX14 4RN

and by Routledge
711 Third Avenue, New York, NY 10017

Routledge is an imprint of the Taylor & Francis Group, an informa business

British Library Cataloguing in Publication Data
A catalogue record for this book is available from the British Library

ISBN: 978-1-138-80870-6 (Set)
ISBN: 978-1-315-18006-9 (Set) (ebk)
ISBN: 978-1-138-28952-9 (Volume 5) (hbk)
ISBN: 978-1-315-26707-4 (Volume 5) (ebk)

Publisher's Note
The publisher has gone to great lengths to ensure the quality of this reprint but
points out that some imperfections in the original copies may be apparent.

Disclaimer
The publisher has made every effort to trace copyright holders and would welcome
correspondence from those they have been unable to trace.

TELECOMMUTING

Modeling the Employer's and the Employee's Decision-Making Process

---

ADRIANA BERNARDINO

GARLAND PUBLISHING, Inc.
New York & London / 1996

Library of Congress Cataloging-in-Publication Data

Bernardino, Adriana, 1961–
    Telecommuting : modeling the employer's and the employee's
decision-making process / Adriana Bernardino.
        p.   cm. — (Garland studies on industrial productivity)
    Includes bibliographical references and index.
    ISBN 0-8153-2723-4 (alk. paper)
    1. Telecommuting—Decision making. 2. Telecommuting—
United States. I. Title. II. Series.
HD2336.3.B47 1996
331.2'5—dc20   96-36710

Printed on acid-free, 250-year-life paper
Manufactured in the United States of America

To Don Levi, my partner in life

Contents

List of Figures

List of Tables

Acknowledgments

This research was conducted at the Massachussets Institute of Technology, under the supervision of Professor Moshe Ben-Akiva, in partial fulfillment of the requirements for the degree of Doctor in Philosophy in Transportation and Decision Sciences.

It was partially supported by the Brazilian Government, through the CNPq - Conselho de Desenvolvimento Científico e Tecnológico - fellowship, by a grant from the NEC Corporation Fund for Research in Computers and Communications to MIT, and by the UPS Doctoral Fellowship.

Telecommuting

I

Introduction

Telecommuting has been regarded as a powerful tool to reduce traffic congestion, pollution and energy consumption. It is supposed to improve lifestyle quality and job satisfaction by providing employees with flexible schedules with which to address their work load and personal requirements. It is further suggested that such arrangements could enhance recruitment capability and productivity, and significantly reduce organization costs. Nevertheless, a strong resistance to the adoption of telecommuting still persists. Managers fear they may lose control over their remote subordinates and employees are concerned they may be socially and professionally isolated.

In this book, state of the art demand modeling techniques are used to delve into critical issues raised by the question of telecommuting. The benefits and costs of telecommuting are investigated, in an effort to provide concrete evidence to inform the private sector's adoption decision process and the public sector's policy design.

As defined herein, telecommuting refers to working arrangements in which the office employee is allowed or required to work from home or from a telework center on a full- or part-time basis, during standard business hours, maintaining contact with the office through telecommunications devices. Telecommuting includes, for example, working from home once a week and communicating with the office via telephone, or working four days a week from a telework center, communicating with the office via electronic mail and telephone.

A behavioral framework, incorporating both the employer's and the employee's perspectives, is conceptualized. Based on this framework, probabilistic choice models are estimated to assess the likelihood of an employer offering a telecommuting program to her/his employees, and of an employee adopting an offered program. This model system is used to forecast the level of adoption of telecommuting under various scenarios and to assess its costs and benefits to the public and private sectors.

THE NEED TO UNDERSTAND TELECOMMUTING

Telecommuting has been regarded as having the potential to address a series of concerns of the public and private sectors, such as traffic congestion, pollution, energy consumption, labor shortage, office space and family commitments. The true extent of this potential needs to be assessed, so that decisions can be made on whether and how to invest in policies to foster the adoption process.

The Public Sector's Perspective

The public sector has demonstrated an increasing interest in the potential of telecommuting, strongly supporting its adoption in numerous public policy statements (Mokhtarian [35]). The primary reason for such interest is that telecommuting appears to address, through the reduction of work trips, a host of transportation issues such as traffic congestion, pollution and energy consumption.

Pendyala et al [46] and Kitamura et al [28] demonstrate empirically that telecommuting significantly reduces commute and peak period trips, total distance traveled and freeway miles. Telecommuters tend to choose non-work destinations closer to home and exhibit a contracted action space on both telecommuting and commuting days.

Hamer et al [22] find that telecommuting can be fairly successful in reducing total travel time of telecommuters. A significant reduction in peak hour car traffic by telecommuters is observed, as well as a decrease in the number of trips for other purposes by both telecommuters and other household members. Henderson et al [23] and Sampath et al [49] empirically demonstrate that telecommuting can have a large effect on daily emissions, with a 50 to 60% decrease in pollutants generated by the telecommuter's vehicle use on telecommuting days. Even though these are very localized projects, based on highly selected samples, the results show travel impacts in the short-term that are favorable enough to justify further interest in the implementation of telecommuting policy as a measure for travel demand management.

Moreover, telecommuting can be implemented now, at relatively low expense for the public sector, since most costs are borne by the employer and/or the employees. It faces no public resistance and addresses a variety of other public sector concerns, such as the integrity of the nuclear family, the employment of individuals with disabilities or with constrained mobility, rural economic development and community involvement (Mokhtarian [35]). As a consequence, the public sector has been very supportive of telecommuting, funding many telecommuting projects during their demonstration phase, together with private partners. A fairly comprehensive description of programs at least partially funded by the public sector is presented in U.S.D.O.T. [13] and International Labour Organization [26].

However, the questions still to be answered are whether the level of telecommuting that can take place is sufficient to have a significant impact on the transportation system and, if such a level of telecommuting may have an impact, what policies can be designed to foster the adoption process.

Previous studies have attempted to quantify the potential adoption of telecommuting (JALA Associates [27], U.S.D.O.T. [13], Boghani et al [4]). However, these studies are based on deterministic assumptions about parameters such as the percentage of the population to whom telecommuting is feasible, the percentage of this population who would adopt telecommuting and the average telecommuting frequency. These assumptions are not based in any behavioral theory. As such, even though these studies define useful boundaries for an expected level of adoption, they provide no information that can guide the public sector in the design of policies to achieve such levels.

Therefore, the development of a more powerful model system, which is based on a behavioral interpretation and includes variables that are policy sensitive is required. The development of such a model system involves the understanding of both the employer's and the employee's perspectives on the adoption process.

The Employer's Perspective

Employers have been facing tremendous challenges in the last decades. The globalization of markets has greatly increased competition, requiring many firms to significantly enhance productivity and/or reduce costs to maintain market share. Moreover, a series of structural changes are forcing organizations to confront new issues that were of no concern previously.

• *LABOR SHORTAGE*

While the global labor pool is growing, the domestic supply of skilled, educated or experienced workers is shrinking. The unwillingness of such employees to relocate to where jobs are known to be available is increasing, reflecting onerous relocation costs, as well as a general unwillingness to submit the family to significant changes for job reasons (Cross and Raizman [9]). As such, in order to maintain a stable, capable work force, an immense effort is required from management.

• *CHANGE IN LABOR FORCE DEMOGRAPHICS*

Dealing with this labor shortage is also leading employers to increasingly depend on women, minorities and physically challenged individuals. This fact, coupled with a change in the characteristics of the American family, is significantly modifying the demographics of the labor force and exacerbating the complexity of the labor issues employers must face.

The number of dual-income and female-headed households has significantly increased in the last few years. Current estimates indicate that about 50% of the labor force belong to dual income households, and some 18% belong to households where a woman is the single earner. Only 19% of the labor force falls into the traditional model of a family in which the man is the single earned (DOL [14]).

Such changes in the family structure are creating a need for support in the household which is currently not available. In particular, the quality and cost of child and elder care available in the US often make them an unfeasible option. Gregory [21] estimated the average annual cost of day care for two children to be nearly one third of the average working woman's income. Consequently, about one fifth of the work force deals with elder care problems, while many in the sandwich generation take care of both children and elder individuals simultaneously (Kugelmass [31]).

- *ABSENTEEISM*

Due primarily to these circumstances, the level of absenteeism has become a major problem for employers in the US. Hours lost to absenteeism have doubled in the last ten years, the equivalent of a 40% increase in the unemployment rate (Kugelmass [31]). This incredible growth has a significant impact on the economy, since for every 0.5% increase in the level of absenteeism, the US gross national product declines by some $10 billion (Dalton and Mesch [10]).

- *DISABLED INDIVIDUALS*

Employers must also be concerned with providing opportunities to individuals with disabilities. About 85% of disabled employable Americans are unemployed. This group constitutes a significant source of labor supply. Moreover, the Americans with Disabilities Act (ADA) reinforces equal employment rights for these individuals. Thus, employers who disregard their working interests can be subject to severe anti-discrimination litigation (Kugelmass [31]).

- *MINORITIES*

Minorities constitute a major source of labor supply. However, this segment of the population is composed primarily of low income households, located in the inner cities of major metropolitan areas in the US. Office based activities, on the other hand, have been increasingly shifting their locations to the suburbs, which are not easily accessible by public transportation (Castells [7]). Transportation costs constitute, then, a major barrier for such individuals to search for and engage in jobs.

- *LOCATION COSTS*

The costs of office and parking spaces in most urban areas is also a major problem faced by organizations. In 1980, the square foot of a suburban office space was priced between $10 and $50, while the square foot of a downtown space was priced between $50 and $100 (Leinberger and Lockwood [32]). Downtown offices could be rented at $18 to $42 per square foot, while suburban offices could be rented at $15 to $24. The annual cost of housing a single worker in a downtown office has recently been estimated to range between $4,000 and $6,000, excluding the cost of electricity, real estate and other taxes (Gordon and Kelly [20]).

• *CONGESTION COSTS*

As a consequence of the high costs of downtown locations, a major process of suburbanization of organizations, and particularly of office activities, has been taking place since the late 1960's in most metropolitan areas in the US. These suburban centers, contrary to their inner-city predecessors, are low density areas, where parking lots are predominant. Such arrangement offers easier access to the labor force than downtown areas (Castells [7]).

However, the massive suburban decentralization of organizations is closely associated with the expansion of the metropolitan freeway system and the use of the automobile as the prevalent mode of commuting (Castells [7]), significantly contributing to increase traffic congestion, air pollution and energy consumption. Nowadays, organizations are being forced to confront their contribution to the deterioration of the environment and the transportation infrastructure, since the Clean Air Act mandates that employers reduce the congestion caused by single occupancy vehicles.

• *THE POTENTIAL OF TELECOMMUTING*

Telecommuting, it has been claimed, is a powerful tool with which to address many of these issues. It may help the employer to respond to employees' demands, to reduce labor costs, to access an expanded labor pool which includes home-bound individuals, to reduce expenditures on office space and location (Nilles [40], Gordon[19], Edwards and Edwards [15], and Olson [43]) and to comply with environmental mandates.

Therefore, many organizations in the US and worldwide are trying telecommuting on both a pilot and a permanent basis. Other organizations are currently in the process of designing a program for their employees. See U.S.D.O.T. [13], Mokhtarian [35], Fritz et al [16] and [17] and International Labour Organization [26] for an update.

Some of these efforts have supported the efficacy of telecommuting in addressing many of these issues. Nevertheless, current management style and corporate culture are still a large barrier to the wider adoption of telecommuting. In large US corporations, the prevailing philosophy of encouraging close employee identification with the organization is considered to be in direct contradiction with the telecommuting philosophy (Olson [42] and [43]).

Similarly, the adoption of team-based structures by some organizations may run against the adoption of telecommuting. The management of remote workers can be very demanding for managers who rely on frequent visual contact for reassurance that their staff is really working, even more so if telecommuters are primarily professional staff, whose productivity is inherently difficult to quantify.

Increasing the level of adoption will, therefore, require presenting employers with convincing evidence of the beneficial impacts of telecommuting. Thus, the effort of quantifying the costs and benefits of adoption must be undertaken.

The Employee's Perspective

Even though the public sector's major focus on telecommuting is aimed at its potential to reduce work trips, the commute may not be the primary reason for an employee to adopt a telecommuting program. Actually, Mokhtarian [35] found no significant relationship between commute length and frequency of telecommuting. Similarly, Bernardino et al [3] found that the impact of commuting time on the decision to adopt telecommuting is not significant.

On the other hand, as mentioned previously, the changing priorities of the labor force are significantly increasing the demand for telecommuting. Many researchers have found that the choice of an alternative lifestyle, as well as socio-economic or physical constraints to mobility, are relevant factors in the decision to telecommute (Olson and Primps [44], Kraut and Grambsch [30], and Bailyn [1]). In particular, the increasing number of women joining the labor force and the change in the shape and size of the traditional family generate the need for more flexible working arrangements.

Currently, approximately 17% of the working women have children under 6 years of age (DOL [14]). Even though telecommuting should not be seen as a substitute for day care, the schedule flexibility it allows contributes significantly to the cohesion of the family.

A significant increase in the home/work conflict, and the consequent opting for a more balanced lifestyle, has been observed, in both men and women. A survey of 1,200 men in a Minneapolis firm indicates that 70% of the employees who are 35 years old or less face serious conflicts between work and family. Many would turn down promotions to avoid increasing work/family conflicts (Kugelmass [31]).

Despite the desire to have a more flexible schedule, the fear that telecommuting will negatively affect promotion, reduce job opportunities and induce social isolation and workaholism may decrease the level of adoption. Therefore, it is important, from the policy-makers' perspective, to understand who potential telecommuters are, and why they would adopt telecommuting, so that policies can be designed accordingly. For example, if the primary goal of an employee is to be able to spend more time with the family, a telework center based telecommuting program would be of no use.

It is also important for the employee to be able to quantify the potential impact of different arrangements on her/his life overall, so that an informed decision can be made. Finally, it would also be in the best interest of the employee to have management support flexible arrangements, which reinforces the need to quantify telecommuting costs and benefits from the managerial perspective.

Urban Travel Demand Models

Recent surveys have demonstrated that the number of telecommuters (full time employees, who would otherwise commute) in the US population has increased significantly in the last few years, from 0.4 million in 1990 to approximately 2.4 million in 1992 (LINK Resources [33]). If one adds to this group contract workers, who worked out of their home at least part time during regular business hours, this number rises to 7.5 million in 1993 (Business Week [6]).

The U.S.D.O.T. [13] estimates that by year 2002 between 7.5 and 15.0 million employees will telecommute an average of 3 to 4 days per week. Mokhtarian [35] assesses that working from home as a commute mode has already reached a share comparable to that of transit in many US cities. Given these estimates, it is necessary to incorporate home-based work in general, and telecommuting in particular, to the traditional urban travel demand forecast system.

A behavioral framework for urban travel forecasting is presented in Figure 1.1. It focuses on the household decisions that lead to a demand for travel, including lifestyle and accessibility, as well as activity and travel scheduling and rescheduling. However, it also incorporates the impacts of the urban and regional development process on household decisions, the effects of these decisions on the performance of the transportation system, and their long-term feedback relationships. Telecommuting affects each and every stage of this process.

It affects urban and regional development decisions by providing organizations with an alternative solution to problems involving labor supply, office space and commuting costs. Telecommuting enables a spatial decentralization process. As a result, households are provided with a much wider range of alternatives to their job selection decisions, which should be incorporated into the forecasting process. Moreover, the availability of telecommuting improves the general accessibility of all regions, increasing the attractiveness of many areas for housing location.

Within the household domain, telecommuting affects both long-term and short-term choices, which will eventually affect the use of the transportation system. Long-term choices concern accessibility and lifestyle. They define the set of activities in which individuals plan to engage and the range of alternative modes which will be available for the performance of these activities. In particular, they include choices of working arrangement, housing location, activity set, automobile ownership and accessibility to information technology alternatives.

The availability of telecommuting influences household members' decision to enter the job market and the choice of working arrangement. The adoption of telecommuting may impact the choice of house characteristics and housing location, potentially influencing urban-sprawl. This aspect of adoption has been of major concern to transportation planners, and some assessments of this long-term impact of telecommuting have been carried out (JALA Associates [27],

Figure 1.1- Travel Demand Forecasting Framework

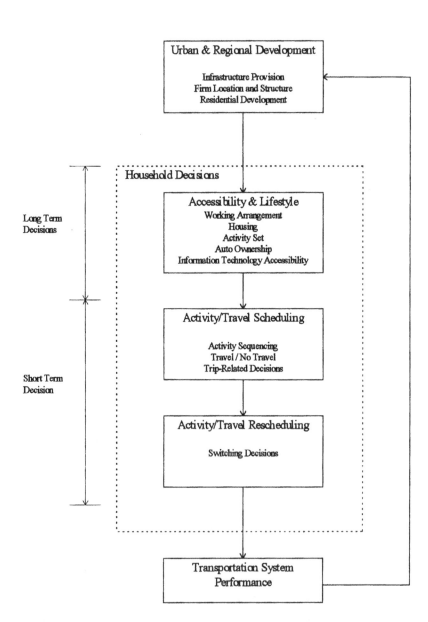

Mokhtarian [35], Nilles [41] and the U.S.D.O.E. [12]). These studies, however, are aggregate estimates with no behavioral basis, providing no information for policy-makers to control undesirable effects.

The adoption of telecommuting may also free up some time and income for engagement in other activities not previously performed. The shift of the primary work location to the house or a telework center may also change the accessibility to various activities, therefore changing the selected activity set. The reduced commuting frequency may decrease the level of automobile ownership. On the other hand, telecommuting may require the purchase of additional equipment or subscription to telecommunications services which would otherwise be dispensable.

Short-term choices involve daily activity selection, scheduling of activities and travel-related decisions. The potential impacts of telecommuting in such decisions has been extensively discussed by Salomon [48], Nilles [40], and Mokhtarian [35]. A reduction in the total number of commuting trips is expected. Consequently, a reduction in peak hour trips, as well as a shift of trip time to off-peak hours, may take place. Carpools may be interrupted, requiring individuals to drive alone. Trip chains may be disrupted. Non-work trips may shift to destinations closer to home, allowing for a shift to non-motorized modes such as walking and biking. A reassignment of activities may be observed in the households, with a transfer of the responsibility for household-related trips to regular commuting members. Furthermore, the availability of dynamic information on the transportation network attributes a dynamic aspect to these decisions. Nevertheless, no transportation behavioral model has been expanded to assess these impacts

Ultimately, telecommuting will affect the performance of the transportation system. As mentioned previously, pilot studies have demonstrated the beneficial short-term impact of telecommuting on the transportation system (Pendyala et al [46], Kitamura et al [28] and Hamer et al [22]). The U.S.D.O.E. [12] indicates that substantially increased levels of telecommuting can reduce traffic delays, motor fuel consumption, highway capacity expansion requirements and pollutant emissions. The study concludes that the energy and emission benefits of telecommuting are not likely to be entirely offset by the replacement of telecommuters by current latent travel demand or by the geographical expansion of cities. However, its demand forecast follows no behavioral theory. As such, it is not possible to assess the sensitivity of the results to structural changes or to telecommuting-related policies. Therefore, a model system that allows for this sensitivity is in order.

The Need to Model the Telecommuting Adoption Process

Given the availability of telecommuting, the household use of urban space and of the transportation system may change dramatically. Individuals are expected to change their travel patterns, including travel time, travel mode and trip destination. The automobile that is not used for commuting may be used for other purposes, eventually increasing the number of automobile trips made by the household. Individuals may consider moving to a more distant location, increasing the urban sprawl. Even though the short-term impact of telecommuting on the transportation system has been proven to be beneficial, the long-term impact is still unknown.

The extent to which this impact is relevant for public policy decisions depends on how much telecommuting will occur. If this volume is large enough to influence the performance of the transportation system and the characteristics of the urban space, it becomes important to understand what the expected impact is. If overall, telecommuting is expected to be beneficial, it is desirable to identify policies that can foster the adoption process. If the overall impact is expected to be negative, it is important to understand how the urban services and infrastructure can be reconfigured so as to mitigate these effects.

The first step in this process, then, is understanding who will telecommute and why. With this understanding, it is possible to forecast how much telecommuting will occur, and how sensitive this demand is to structural changes and policies. Achieving this objective requires using a behavioral approach to model the adoption decision process.

CONTRIBUTION

In this book a model system is developed to explain the process and forecast the level of adoption of telecommuting. This model system is instrumental to the design of public and private policies that impact the adoption process and to the decision-making of the public sector, employers and employees, to the extent that it

- provides an assessment of the costs and benefits of telecommuting from the perspectives of employers, employees and policy-makers;
- is based on a behavioral framework;
- includes policy sensitive variables; and
- is consistent with the urban travel demand modeling framework.

In the behavioral framework developed and demonstrated here the employer is assumed to have a profit maximization behavior and the employee is assumed to have a utility maximizing behavior. Given these assumptions, the design of a telecommuting program is modeled as a function of the motivations and constraints faced by the organization, and the employer's decision to make telecommuting available is modeled as a function of the expected impacts of the designed program on productivity and costs. The employee's choice of a telecommuting program is modeled as a function of her/his motivations and constraints, and the decision to adopt telecommuting as a function of the potential impacts of the program on the employee's lifestyle, work-related costs and income.

In the stated preference survey conducted with various US organizations, both employers and employees are required to make decisions about all the aspects involved in designing a telecommuting program, so they can experience the actual complexity of the adoption decision process in their choice tasks. To create a more realistic choice context, both employers and employees are given the opportunity to design their preferred telecommuting program, rather than only being presented with alternatives designed by the researcher.

State-of-the-art demand modeling techniques are used to devise comprehensive measures for the impact of a telecommuting arrangement on (i) productivity, incorporating individual and group productivity, as well as supervisory capabilities, (ii) the organization's costs, including equipment, telecommunication, overhead and employee direct and indirect costs, (iii) the employee's lifestyle quality, including career, family and social life, and (iv) the employee's working costs, including transportation, telecommunications, liabilities, home utilities and child care expenses.

It is demonstrated that the ideal telecommuting program depends on the characteristics of the organization and on the employer's motivations and constraints to adopt telecommuting. For example, small organizations prefer a program with a flexible schedule, while large organizations prefer a fixed telecommuting schedule. Organizations seeking to address employees' needs are more likely to offer flexible telecommuting arrangements than organizations looking for a cost reduction.

It is demonstrated that the impact of telecommuting on productivity is a function of the flexibility that is provided to the employee to address her/his work load and personal needs. It is also shown that the potential of telecommuting to reduce an organization's costs is limited, unless a large enough number of employees telecommute often enough to free some office space. An overall negative perception of telework centers among employers is identified.

It is demonstrated that the impact of telecommuting on lifestyle depends on the characteristics of the employee and of her/his job. For example, parents of young children are more likely to perceive an improvement in lifestyle quality due to telecommuting than individuals with no young children. Individuals working primarily on a team perceive more beneficial impacts of telecommuting on lifestyle than individuals working primarily on individual tasks. A negative attitude toward telework centers among employees is identified.

Various telecommuting policies are tested and guidelines are provided for both the public and the private sectors to foster the adoption process. It is demonstrated that the need to address the employees' needs is one of the major motivations for adoption of telecommuting. An increase in the level of information about telecommuting available to employers, in conjunction with the design of programs that actually address employees' needs may increase adoption significantly. Differences in an organization's scale and structure do not significantly impact the level of adoption, but change the characteristics of the available programs.

OUTLINE

The remainder of this book is divided into six chapters. Chapter 2 presents a review of the state of the art of modeling the telecommuting adoption process. Chapter 3 discusses the proposed modeling framework and compares it with the state of the art. Chapter 4 describes the surveys used to collect the data to estimate the proposed models and presents the descriptive statistics of the sample. Chapter 5 presents the model structure and the estimation results. Chapter 6 provides an assessment of the level of adoption of telecommuting and an evaluation of various public and private policies intended to foster the adoption process. Chapter 7 concludes the study and discusses directions for further research.

II

The State-of-the-Art

Previous behavioral research on the process of adoption of telecommuting has helped to define the context within which this book is developed. In this chapter, a discussion of existing research on the employer's and the employee's decision processes is presented.

THE EMPLOYER'S DECISION PROCESS

Existing research on the employer's decision process is largely qualitative, and focuses on the motivations for employers to offer telecommuting and on managers' attitudes towards telecommuting. See, for example, Nilles [40], Gordon[19], Edwards and Edwards [15], and Olson [43].

Fritz et al [16] and [17] propose a general framework to assess the suitability of telework for an organization before an assessment of the costs and benefits of adoption is performed. The authors suggest that the organization should first determine the motivation to adopt telecommuting. If there is sufficient motivation, the job functions or processes to be subjected to telecommuting should be identified. The behavioral characteristics of the related employees and the suitability of these functions and processes to telecommuting, should be assessed. If jobs and processes are not suitable to telecommuting, the possibility of redesigning functions should be considered. If employees do not present the necessary behavioral characteristics, the possibility of educating the labor force should be evaluated. If both the job and the labor force adequacy conditions are in place, telecommuting is suitable for the organization, and a feasibility study should then take place. A similar decision process is suggested by other authors. See, for example, Gordon and Kelly [20].

Bernardino et al [3] suggest an overall analytical framework for the adoption process, in which the employer's characteristics influence the employee's adoption decision. The authors identify the employer's decision to offer a program as being a function of the organizational characteristics, including the composition of the labor force, organizational costs and organizational structure, as well as of the managers' attitudes toward and perceptions of telecommuting.

Sullivan et al [51] propose a comprehensive analytical framework for the adoption process. In this framework, the environment, the manager's characteristics and the organizational characteristics influence the organization's considerations with regard to implementing telecommuting. The organization's preference for telecommuting, in turn, is influenced by these considerations, in addition to organizational and job characteristics. Given the organization's preferences and existing situational constraints, a choice is made whether to make telecommuting available. The employee's choice to telecommute is constrained by the organization's decision to make a program available. Collectively, employees' choices determine the impact of adoption on the transportation system.

Based on this framework, Yen et al [52] design a survey and present an exploratory analysis of the data collected from 83 executives. The survey includes questions about the organization and the respondent's characteristics, as well as the respondent's attitudes towards telecommuting and the stated preference to support different program scenarios proposed by the researchers.

The attitudinal questions refer to the expected impacts of telecommuting on telecommuters, non-telecommuters and workers overall, and on the public image of the organization and on managerial effectiveness. The exploratory analysis of the responses indicates that, on average, respondents expect telecommuting to help increase employee retention and recruitment, as well as telecommuters' morale. A small portion of the sample expects telecommuting to increase telecommuters' productivity. The majority expects a negative impact on non-telecommuters' morale and productivity, as well as a negative impact on managers' ability to supervise telecommuters.

No socio-economic characteristics of the respondents are highly correlated with these attitudes. Attitudes are primarily influenced by management style. In particular, respondents who, as a method of supervision, assess the final accomplishment of employees, rather than employee presence in the office, have a more positive attitude towards telecommuting. Familiarity with telecommuting and current availability of a telecommuting program positively impact respondents' attitudes.

In the stated preference exercise respondents are presented with nine scenarios composed of changing levels in a telecommuter's salary and levels of telecommuting costs borne by the organization. A salary can be 5% lower, the same or 5% higher than that currently paid to the employee. Telecommuting costs can be totally, partially or not borne by the employer. Respondents are then asked if they would definitely, possibly or not support the proposed telecommuting scenario.

An analysis of the frequency of responses to each scenario identifies that less than 10% of the respondents would support telecommuting under any circumstances, while about 33% would never support it. Under the *status quo* scenario, in which telecommuter's salary is the same and the employer incurs no extra cost, the answers are equally distributed among the three possible alternatives. A salary decrease is unanimously rejected as a definitive option. Some employers would accept a salary increase, but the majority would reject this alternative.

As the fraction of the telecommuting costs borne by the employer increases, the preference for the telecommuting arrangement decreases, as expected. The variables that seem to influence the employer's preferences are telecommuting awareness, computer penetration and management characteristics. In particular, managers supervising up to six employees, and at lower ranks in the organizational hierarchy favor telecommuting more than other managers.

No estimation of the stated preference model is provided. However, based on this exploratory analysis, the authors conclude that in order to increase the level of adoption an increase is needed in the amount of information about telecommuting available to organizations and management concerns about telecommuting impacts on productivity, ability to supervise and data security need to be alleviated.

THE EMPLOYEE'S DECISION PROCESS

Even though only a small number of behavioral studies have been conducted on the employee's decision process, it nevertheless has been more fully explored than the employer's perspective. In this section, behavioral frameworks, qualitative data analyses and behavioral models are discussed.

Behavioral Frameworks

Sullivan et al [51] propose a framework in which the employee's preference for telecommuting is a function of her/his perceptions, as well as of her/his individual and job characteristics. The choice to adopt telecommuting is a function of these preferences, as well as of the program availability and of situational constraints.

Bernardino et al [3] characterize the employee's decision to telecommute as a two stage process, which includes the telecommuting adoption and telecommuting frequency choices. The authors define a telecommuting program as a combination of various attributes, including program formality, telecommuting place, schedule flexibility, employment conditions, fixed and operating costs and liability. The employee's choice to adopt telecommuting is conditional on the employer offering the option, and influenced by the characteristics of the offered arrangement, as well as by situational issues, including job, commuting and socio-economic-demographic characteristics.

Mokhtarian and Salomon [36] develop a conceptual model of the employee's decision process that explicitly incorporates three major elements to the choice context: constraints, facilitators and drives. While constraints prevent or hinder telecommuting adoption, facilitators allow or favor the change. Constraints are classified into external and internal. External constraints can be directly addressed by policies, and relate to telecommuting awareness and job characteristics. Internal constraints involve psycho-social aspects, including personal interaction needs, household interaction problems, lack of discipline and risk aversion. The absence of constraints is a necessary, but not a sufficient condition for the adoption of telecommuting. Drives which motivate the employee must be present for adoption to take place.

Qualitative Data Analyses

Mahmassani et al [34] present an exploratory analysis of the data from an employee survey conducted as part of the effort to model the analytical framework presented by Sullivan et al [51]. The survey collected data about the respondents' job, commuting and socio-economic characteristics, as well as attitudes towards telecommuting and the stated preference for telecommuting scenarios proposed by the researchers.

In the stated preference task respondents are presented with seven different scenarios combining various levels of salary and telecommuting costs borne by the employees. The salary can be 10% or 5% lower, the same, or 5% higher than that currently paid to the employee. Telecommuting costs can include acquiring a new telephone line or a personal computer. Other options are that the costs be totally borne by the employee, partially borne by the employer, or totally borne by the employer. Under each scenario, the respondents are asked if they would prefer to telecommute from home every day, telecommute from home several days a week, possibly telecommute from home or not telecommute.

An analysis of the frequency of the responses to each scenario indicates that 15% of the respondents would prefer to telecommute under any circumstance, while other 15% would never prefer to telecommute. Incurring some telecommuting cost is more acceptable than a salary decrease. A salary increase is not as significant an incentive as a salary decrease is a deterrent of adoption.

Computer proficiency, computer ownership, long commuting distance and long commuting time have a positive effect on employee's preference for telecommuting. Current telecommuters, females and employees in non-managerial positions are more likely to prefer telecommuting than the average respondent.

Bernardino et al [3] conduct a survey to collect data on the employees' motivations and perceived barriers to the adoption of telecommuting, as well as on their stated preferences for telecommuting scenarios proposed by the researchers. The survey is distributed to users of various computer network groups.

An analysis of the data indicates that employees perceive telecommuting to increase schedule flexibility, productivity and autonomy. It is also perceived to reduce commuting stress and family/work conflict, and to have no significant impact on job promotion, working costs and the employee's isolation.

The main perceived barriers to further adoption of telecommuting by their employing organization are the cultural requirement of conventional 9-to-5 office hours and the fact that interactions through telecommunications media are not as efficient as face-to-face interactions.

Mokhtarian and Salomon [37] examine the relationship among the possibility, the preference and the choice to adopt home- based telecommuting for a sample of 628 City of San Diego employees. The authors define three external dichotomous constraints to the adoption choice: lack of awareness, job unsuitability and manager disapproval. They observe that for 71% of the sample at least one of these constraints is binding. Lack of awareness, job unsuitability and manager disapproval are binding constraints for respectively 21%, 34% and 48% of the sample, again demonstrating management resistance as the most frequent impediment to adoption of telecommuting. For about 60% of the surveyed employees, telecommuting is the preferred unavailable alternative, given these binding constraints.

Among those respondents for whom none of the above constraints is binding, about 50% do not choose telecommuting, according to the authors, due to the presence of active internal constraints. For only 12% of the sample is telecommuting possible, preferred and the chosen alternative. Telecommuting is a not-preferred, available alternative for 14.6%, and neither preferred, nor available for 46.3% of the sample.

Behavioral Models

Sullivan et al [51] develop a model of employees' stated preferences for adoption of telecommuting in a cost neutral scenario. Under this scenario, all telecommuting costs are incurred by the employer and the telecommuter's salary remains the same. The authors' objective with such a model is to relate the employee's stated preference to individual and household characteristics, work and work-related attributes, and travel-related variables.

The estimation results indicate that as the round-trip commuting time increases, employees are more likely to prefer to telecommute full-time, if the total travel time is 20 minutes and over. The more commute stops per week an employee makes, the higher her/his probability of preferring to telecommute full- or part-time, probably indicating the desire for more flexibility to combine work with other activities.

If the employee has been working in the same organization for five or more years, her/his preference for telecommuting is smaller than that of employees who have joined the organization more recently. If the employee works on a computer for at least four hours a day, her/his preference for full-time telecommuting increases. On the other hand, if the employee makes several daily face-to-face contacts with customers, coworkers and supervisors to perform her/his tasks, the preference for full-time telecommuting decreases.

Females with young children have a higher preference for telecommuting than the average respondent. Male workers belonging to households with an annual income lower than $25,000 dollars have higher preference for full-time telecommuting, indicating the high impact of working costs on low-income household members' decision to participate in the labor force.

Bernardino et al [3] develop a model of the employee's stated preference for various telecommuting scenarios. In each scenario, the employee is presented with a different combination of telecommuting frequency, schedule flexibility, salary, available equipment and cost responsibilities for a home-based program. The respondents are required to state their preferences in a scale from (1), "would definitely not telecommute," to (5), "would definitely telecommute."

The estimated model can only capture the significance of the attributes of the telecommuting arrangements related to telecommuting costs and salary. In particular, if employees are required to provide a computer or pay for work-related phone bills, the probability of adoption decreases. Similarly, the probability of adoption decreases if telecommuters are not paid for overtime work hours. However, incurring some or all of the telecommuting costs is more acceptable than a salary decrease. Finally, a salary decrease is more of an impediment to adoption than a salary increase is a stimulus.

Parents of children under 18 years old are more likely to prefer telecommuting than the other individuals in the sample. However, commuting time, years of employment in the organization and gender have no significant impact on respondents' preferences. Employees for whom a telecommuting program is currently not available are more likely to prefer telecommuting than those who have the telecommuting choice.

Mokhtarian and Salomon [38] estimate a model of employees' preferences for telecommuting. The authors identify 64 drives, constraints and facilitators that constitute the set of potential explanatory variables for preferences and choices. These variables include attitude measurements, as well as socio-demographic and other objective characteristics. It is demonstrated that drives related to family, independence, leisure, ideology, work and commute make a significant contribution to the formation of employees' preference for telecommuting.

In a further development of this study, Mokhtarian and Salomon [39] estimate a model of the employee's choice to telecommute, based on revealed preference data. The authors demonstrate the significance of preferences, drives, facilitators and constraints in the employees' decision. In particular, the lack of management support is the primary constraint to adoption, followed by job unsuitability. Misunderstanding about what telecommuting is, technology unavailability and lack of discipline are also significant constraints, but with a less dramatic impact. The only significant drives are related to work and commute stress.

The model results are used to evaluate the sensitivity of the demand to the removal of those constraints which can be addressed by policies. It is verified that if the constraints related to unawareness and lack of management support are removed, 13% of the employees for whom telecommuting is the preferred impossible alternative choose to telecommute. If, in addition to that, the job unsuitability constraint is removed, 28% of that group choose to telecommute.

ASSESSING THE STATE-OF-THE-ART

To date, limited behavioral analyses of the telecommuting adoption process have been conducted. Existing research on the employer's perspective has been largely qualitative, with restricted potential for generalization. The research focuses primarily on the motivations that lead employers to offer telecommuting as an alternative working arrangement and on managers' attitudes towards telecommuting.

It has been demonstrated that management style, through its influence on managers' attitudes towards telecommuting, has a significant impact on the decision to make a program available. A lack of interest has been shown by employers in using telecommuting as a means to reduce direct labor costs. Employers' unwillingness to incur significant costs to offer a program has also been observed.

Nevertheless, critical advances in this area of research are still to be made before the employer's decision process can be clearly understood. For example, previous research considers only partial profiles of telecommuting arrangements, concentrating primarily on the impacts of changes in salary and cost levels on the decision to make a program available. The decision to offer telecommuting, however, is far more complex. It involves determining the adequate combination of telecommuting schedule, equipment availability, liabilities and telecommuting place to address each specific set of motivations. It entails assessing the impacts of different arrangements on productivity, on various levels of the organization's costs and on managerial capabilities. It requires comparing telecommuting with other potential alternatives. Previous research does not address any of these issues. This information, however, can be particularly useful in understanding and fostering the adoption process.

Research on the employee's perspective has advanced further, but is still limited. The major concern so far has been with identifying motivations and constraints to the adoption process. It has been demonstrated that an employee's willingness to telecommute is not exclusively a function of individual characteristics and attitudes, but actually depends more on the characteristics of the arrangement. Therefore, organizations can make telecommuting programs more or less attractive to their employees.

However, the efforts undertaken to assess the trade-offs made by employees when considering a telecommuting arrangement have been limited to a partial profile of telecommuting, including only a few aspects related to transportation and work-related costs. No effort has been made to quantify the potential effects of different telecommuting arrangements on generalized working costs or on an employee's lifestyle as a whole.

Moreover, the employer's decision to make a program available is a function, among other factors, of the characteristics of the labor force. The employee's decision to adopt telecommuting depends on the characteristics of the organization, and rests on the offer of a telecommuting program by the employer. Therefore, in order to correctly predict how much telecommuting will occur, a comprehensive model of the adoption process, which explains the behavior of both the employer and the employee, must be used. This model is conceptualized in the next chapter.

III

Analytical Framework

In this chapter, the analytical framework for modeling the telecommuting adoption process is formulated. The main hypotheses concerning both the employer's and the employee's behaviors are discussed.

An outline of the overall framework is presented in Figure 3.1. In the initial stage, the employer identifies motivations for and constraints to the implementation of a telecommuting program and evaluates alternative program designs that satisfy these objectives and constraints. The set of motivations includes the employee's request to telecommute. Those programs which yield higher net benefit to the organization than the conventional commuting situation may be made available to the employees.

If the employer decides to offer a program, the employee may choose to adopt telecommuting. This decision depends on the employee's motivations, as well as on the characteristics of the proposed program. Given her/his motivations and constraints, the employee selects, from the set of all arrangements made available by the employer, the one which best addresses her/his needs. She/he then assesses the net benefits she/he may attain from the selected program and decides to adopt telecommuting if these net benefits are positive.

After some experience with telecommuting, the employer decides whether to maintain, withdraw, or change the characteristics of the program and the employee decides whether to maintain or withdraw from participating.

Figure 3.1 - Telecommuting Adoption Process - Analytical Framework

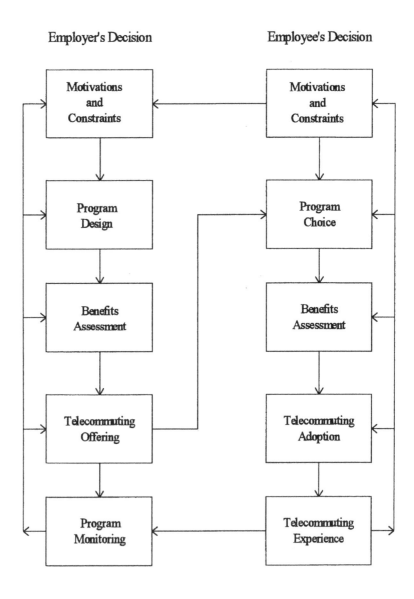

In the following sections, the hypotheses about each stage of this process are detailed. Before these hypotheses can be discussed, however, a clearer definition of telecommuting is in order. This definition is presented next.

DEFINING TELECOMMUTING

As defined in Chapter 1. *telecommuting refers to working arrangements in which the office worker is allowed or required to work from home or from a telework center on a full- or part-time basis, during standard business hours, maintaining contact with the office through telecommunications devices.*

This basic definition distinguishes telecommuting from the broader set of work-at-home arrangements, to the extent that it:

- limits telecommuting to office employees, therefore eliminating self-employed or contracted individuals, non-paid workers and employees that do not work in office related activities, and

- restricts the telecommuting time to regular business hours, thus excluding employees who work from home after hours.

However, the complexity of the characteristics of a telecommuting program requires a more complete definition. It encompasses a host of attributes that can assume various values, with the common characteristic that work is performed remotely from a supervision perspective. Implementing a telecommuting program involves defining:

- *minimum telecommuting days per week required*: Depending on the employer's motivation to implement a telecommuting program, a minimum weekly telecommuting frequency may be required. This could be the case, for example, when the employer is trying to comply with traffic reduction mandates.

- *maximum telecommuting days per week allowed*: As a matter of control or practicality, the employer may want to limit the maximum number of days an individual can telecommute each week.

- *telecommuting schedule flexibility*: The telecommuting schedule may be so rigid that it specifies the days of the week in which telecommuting is required or allowed, or it can be flexible, allowing a selection of telecommuting days that satisfies both the employee's and the employer's demands.

- *office space available for commuting days*: Telecommuting differs from regular commuting arrangements in its requirement of space for the employee in the organization's office. As such, the employer needs to decide whether the telecommuter will be provided with an individual office, a shared office or a shared desk to work at on commuting days.

- *telecommuter's salary*: In some situations, the employee may be willing to trade some salary for the possibility of working at home. In other circumstances, the employer may be willing to provide a monetary incentive to encourage telecommuting. Thus, the employer needs to decide whether the salary paid to telecommuters will be higher, lower or the same as the salary they are paid as regular commuters.

- *telecommuting place*: Telecommuting can take place from home or from a telework center, which is generally a third-party owned facility located closer to the employee's home than the organization's office. Each of these telecommuting sites involves different costs and benefits. The employer needs to assess which place better addresses her/his motivations for considering telecommuting.

- *equipment required for the remote office*: The equipment required for telecommuting to be functional needs to be determined. This includes assessing the need for computers, fax machines, dedicated phone lines, access to a computer network and alike.

- *costs responsibilities*: Implementing a telecommuting program involves incurring in start up, as well as in operating costs. Start up costs include equipment provision and general office setup. Operating costs include primarily expenditures on telecommunications. These costs can be paid by the employer, by the employee, or otherwise shared.

- *liabilities*: Particularly for home-based arrangements, some issues regarding the liability for property and employee safety may arise. These issues must be addressed by the employer, and may include some extra expenditures on insurance.

Given these definitions, the analysis of the adoption process may proceed.

THE EMPLOYER'S DECISION PROCESS

A detailed structure of the employer's decision process is presented in Figure 3.2. The underlying assumption of this process is that the employer's objective is to maximize the organization's profit. The working arrangements offered to the employees she/he supervises are designed so as to attain this objective.

Given this assumption, and presuming the employer has a motivation to consider telecommuting, the offering decision process can be divided into two major stages: program design and the program offering decision. In the first stage, the employer generates telecommuting arrangements which could effectively address her/his motivations to implement a telecommuting program, while satisfying the existing constraints. In the second stage, the employer decides whether or not to offer some or all of the generated arrangements to the employees, based on the assessment of the programs' impact on productivity and costs. These stages are further discussed below.

Program Design

As discussed in Chapter 1, telecommuting is an innovative working arrangement which presents new opportunities for an increase in productivity, access to an expanded labor force, reduction in employee turnover and a decrease in costs. It is assumed that the employer's decision to offer a telecommuting program to her/his employees is derived from the need to address one or more of these issues.

Figure 3.2 - The Employer's Decision Process - Analytical Framework

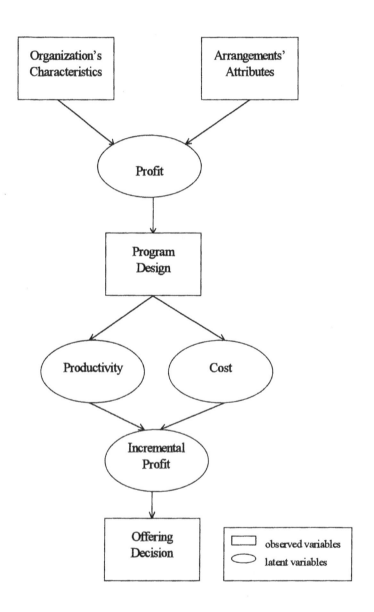

Let the motivations to consider telecommuting be classified into three major groups, according to whether they relate to the need to increase productivity, reduce costs or address employees' requests. The employer needs not be confined to a single group. However, each group will influence the design of the telecommuting arrangement differently.

Specifically, if the employer is motivated primarily by the need to reduce costs, she/he may be inclined to determine a minimum telecommuting frequency and a fixed telecommuting schedule, so that the use of the office space can be optimized. She/he is likely to offer telecommuters a shared desk to work on regular commuting days. She/he may consider paying telecommuters a lower salary than that paid to regular commuters, if trying to reduce labor costs. Alternatively, she/he may offer a salary incentive to telecommuters if the major objective is to reduce office space costs. Moreover, she/he may tend to transfer all the telecommuting costs, including equipment, phone bills and liability, to the employee.

If the primary motivation is the need to increase productivity, the employer is likely to offer a program with a more flexible schedule, which can be adjusted to address the work load and the employee's personal needs. She/he will make sure that all the necessary equipment required for telecommuting to be functional is provided, and will pay for all start up and operating costs. She/he is also likely to pay telecommuters the same salary they are paid as regular employees.

When the employer considers telecommuting to address employees' needs, her/his main objective is to avoid turnover. Therefore, she/he will try to benefit the employee by offering a flexible schedule, paying for all the telecommuting costs and maintaining the employee's salary, in a similar manner to employers seeking to increase productivity.

The employer's selection of the arrangement to address these motivations, however, is constrained by the characteristics of the organization. In particular, the organization's structure and scale are expected to influence the program design.

As far as the structure is concerned, if the employees work primarily in teams, the maximum feasible telecommuting frequency is likely to be restricted. Moreover, flexibility is a major requirement, so that individual preferences can be adjusted to the group needs. Therefore, the employer would be unlikely to design a program that requires a minimum frequency or to define a fixed telecommuting schedule. She/he would be likely to set a low limit to the maximum frequency allowed. If employees work primarily on individual tasks, there are no structural constraints on the feasible telecommuting frequency, and schedule flexibility is not a major requirement. As such, the employer has more freedom to design the program, and can benefit from both a productivity increase and a cost reduction.

Regarding the scale, larger organizations are expected to be more observant of schedules and to function under a more rigid organizational structure than small organizations. Thus, an employer from a large organization is expected to offer more rigid arrangements, overall, than an employer from a small organization.

In general, employers are expected to prefer home to telework center-based telecommuting, since home-based programs have a greater potential for cost reductions and the telework center environment does not differ significantly from the organization's office, as far as productivity is concerned.

The design process involves an assessment of the potential of each telecommuting arrangement to address the employer's motivations and constraints, and the choice of a set of arrangements that fulfill these requirements. Once these telecommuting arrangements have been selected, the employer will compare them to the prevailing arrangement to decide whether to offer all, some or none of them to her/his employees. This decision is discussed next.

Program Offering Decision

The employer may choose to offer one, some or all of the alternative telecommuting arrangements to her/his employees if she/he expects the organization to achieve a higher profit level under any of these arrangements than under the conventional commuting arrangement. Therefore, the employer needs to assess the program's impact on revenue and on costs.

- *IMPACT ON REVENUE*

Assuming that the total number of employees in the organization remains constant, and that there is no change in prices due to the adoption of telecommuting, changes in revenue occur as a consequence of changes in productivity. Changes in productivity may occur at the level of the individual telecommuter, at the level of the team in which the telecommuter participates and at the supervisory level, to the extent that the program affects the manager's capability to supervise and evaluate the telecommuter's work. The assessment of the overall change in productivity is based on changes in all of these levels.

When the outcome of the employee's work can be quantified by a well defined measure, changes in productivity can be easily assessed. However, most of the tasks performed by *white collar* workers are not easily quantified, and assessing changes in productivity can be a major task. While it does depend on the characteristics of the arrangement, it is also, to a great extent, a matter of the employer's perceptions.

As far as the arrangement characteristics are concerned, it is hypothesized that the employer expects the variables associated with telecommuting schedule and place, and with the telecommuter's salary to have a significant impact on productivity. Equipment availability is assumed to be a requirement that needs to be satisfied, rather than a device to increase productivity.

It is hypothesize that establishing a minimum number of days in which telecommuting is required reduces the employee's flexibility in defining her/his working schedule, and therefore generates less satisfaction than if no minimum frequency is required. Moreover, as the minimum number of telecommuting days required increases, a decrease in group productivity and monitoring capabilities should be expected, since the prolonged absence of the telecommuters from the office would reduce the frequency of their face-to-face interactions with coworkers and supervisors. Thus the requirement of a minimum telecommuting frequency is expected to have a negative impact on productivity.

The flexibility a telecommuter has with which to tailor her/his telecommuting program to her/his needs increases as the maximum number of days in which telecommuting is allowed increases. An increase in job satisfaction, and therefore in individual productivity, is then expected. If the allowed telecommuting frequency is high, a prolonged absence from the office may reduce group productivity and monitoring capability. However, if the employees work primarily on individual tasks, the aspects related to individual productivity are expected to prevail and an increase in the maximum number of days in which telecommuting is allowed should have an overall positive impact on productivity.

A flexible telecommuting schedule favors individual and group productivity, as well as monitoring capability, to the extent that it allows for better adjustment of telecommuting days to personal needs and to work load demand. Paying a telecommuter a lower salary than that paid to a regular commuter may generate dissatisfaction, therefore reducing individual productivity. This impact may be indirectly reflected on group productivity, but no significant effect is expected on monitoring capability. Finally, telework center-based telecommuting is expected to have a negative impact on productivity, since it neither provides the support of the organization's office nor the amenities of home.

Regarding the characteristics of the organization, it is hypothesized that if the organization is located in an urban area where traffic congestion is a major issue, the commuting burden may have a negative impact on employee productivity. Therefore, a telecommuting program may be perceived as an efficient tool for increasing productivity. It is hypothesized that the employer's perceptions about the potential of telecommuting to increase productivity varies between industries due to particularities of their market, structure and labor force. These perceptions are also affected by the level of employees' interest in telecommuting.

- *IMPACT ON COSTS*

Changes in costs include the program start-up costs and variations in direct costs per employee, employee turnover costs and overhead costs. Direct costs per employee refer to the wage and benefits awarded to the employees, as well as to expenditures on telecommunications and equipment. Changes in employee turnover cost may occur when telecommuting is adopted to respond to employees' demand. To the extent that this demand is satisfied, telecommuting may reduce annual training and recruiting costs by reducing the employee turnover rate.

Overhead costs include primarily expenditures associated with the use of office space. Office space expenses refer to the costs of housing a single worker in an office, including electricity, real estate and other taxes. Savings in these costs accrue only when a sufficiently high number of staff is telecommuting to allow for a part of a building to be vacant or sublet, or to avoid a move to larger premises. If telecommuting takes place from a telework center, office costs may reappear, even though in a scaled-down form, as overhead costs for the decentralized office.

Start-up costs are the initial expenditures involved in the implementation of the telecommuting program. They represent investments on managers', telecommuters' and coworkers' training, installation of telecommunications links, and any necessary adaptation to the remote work site to make it adequate for the telecommuter. If telework centers are being set up by the organization itself, the expenditure in acquiring or renting the new premises must be added to the start-up costs.

The extent to which telecommuting can influence costs varies with the organization's scale and the characteristics of the labor force. It is expected that large organizations will be less sensitive to changes in costs. Also if there is a demand from the employees to telecommute, turnover costs may be expected to decrease.

The employer evaluates the benefits and costs of the telecommuting program, compares them to those yielded by the conventional commuting arrangement and chooses the arrangement which yields higher profit.

THE EMPLOYEE'S DECISION PROCESS

The employee's decision process is presented in greater detail in Figure 3.3. The underlying assumption in this framework is that the employee maximizes utility. Thus, assuming she/he has a motivation to adopt telecommuting, she/he chooses, from among all the arrangements offered by the employer, the one that maximizes her/his utility, given her/his motivations and situational constraints. The adoption decision process is divided into two stages: program choice and adoption decision.

Program Choice

An employee may consider adopting telecommuting because of lifestyle preferences or to situational constraints. For example, she/he may value a balanced lifestyle more than career achievements, or she/he

Figure 3.3 - The Employee's Decision Process - Analytical Framework

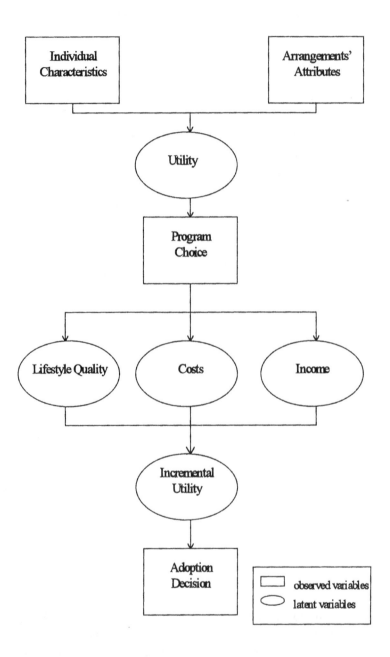

may be a single parent of a young child, with a high demand for schedule flexibility. Given the source of motivation, the employee selects for consideration, from the set of all arrangements made available by the employer, the ones that address her/his needs.

Given the utility maximization assumption, an increase in flexibility is expected to increase the preference for the arrangement, while an increase in costs decreases the preference. Some differences in sensitivity to each of these attributes may be perceived by different groups of individuals. In particular, it is expected that single parents of young children will have a higher demand for flexibility than other employees, thus having a higher willingness to pay for increased flexibility. However, the extent to which an employee is willing to incur costs in telecommuting depends on how much these costs affect her/his available income. Finally, the characteristics of the job, particularly the required amount of face-to-face interactions, may limit the feasible telecommuting frequency, and this aspect is assumed to be factored into the employee's considerations.

Program Adoption Decision

It is assumed that the adoption of telecommuting may affect the employee's utility through the potential impact of the program on her/his lifestyle, work related costs and income.

- *IMPACT ON LIFESTYLE*

Changes in lifestyle encompass changes in personal life and career. They may occur as a consequence of a shift in the amount of time the employee spends in the office and at home and in the amount of time she/he has available to spend in activities other than work.

As far as the arrangement characteristics are concerned, the expected impact of telecommuting on lifestyle quality is hypothesized to be a function of the allowed telecommuting frequency, the flexibility the employee is given to decide on her/his telecommuting schedule and the telecommuting site.

If a minimum telecommuting frequency is required, the telecommuter's flexibility in establishing her/his own schedule will be restricted, and the impact of such a constraint on lifestyle quality will be negative, if compared to a situation in which no lower limit is set on the telecommuting frequency. If an employee is required to telecommute from home many days per week, she/he may attain an increase in productivity from being able to concentrate better. However, she/he may perceive her/his frequent absence from the office as having a negative impact on her/his opportunities for promotion and job security if she/he believes her/his supervisor evaluates employees based on their presence in the office. Overall, as the minimum telecommuting frequency required increases, a negative impact on lifestyle quality is expected.

The higher the number of telecommuting days allowed, the higher the flexibility the telecommuter has with which to arrange her/his work and personal schedules. Therefore, a positive impact on lifestyle quality is expected as the maximum allowed frequency increases. For similar reasons, a flexible telecommuting schedule is expected to have a positive impact on lifestyle quality.

Telework center-based telecommuting is expected to have a negative impact on the employee's lifestyle. It is hypothesized that telework centers are primarily perceived to remove the employee from the organization's environment without providing her/him with more time to socialize with the family.

Regarding individual and household characteristics, it is assumed that females expect a higher improvement in lifestyle quality due to telecommuting than males. If the employee is the parent of a child of pre-school age, lifestyle quality is likely to increase with telecommuting. As the household size increases, telecommuting is expected to decrease lifestyle quality, since the home environment may be inappropriate for work.

Age is expected to have a mixed effect on the perceived impact of telecommuting. Older individuals are likely to be well-established in their careers, and seeking a more balanced lifestyle. On the other hand, precisely due to the progression of their careers, they are likely to have achieved a level of flexibility in their schedules that does not require a formal telecommuting program. Young individuals may appreciate the flexibility allowed by telecommuting, but feel the need to be constantly present in the work environment to achieve higher promotions.

Managers and professionals are expected to perceive less improvement in lifestyle than administrative support staff, since the latter are likely to have a more rigid working schedule. The amount of team work performed by an individual may also influence the perceptions of the impact of telecommuting on lifestyle. Finally, the longer the employee's commuting trip, the higher the expected improvement in lifestyle quality due to telecommuting.

• *IMPACT ON COSTS*

Work-related costs may change due to variations in expenditures on equipment, phone bills, transportation, home utilities, insurance, and child and elder care. It is assumed that if the employee were to telecommute from home many days per week, she/he would expect an increase in the cost of home utilities, such as heat and electricity, particularly if the premises were otherwise not used during business hours. However, the larger the employee's household, the more likely that the home premises would be used during business hours, irrespective of the employee enrolling in a telecommuting program. Therefore, the increase in the expenses of home utilities would not be so significant.

An increase in the working costs is to be expected if the employee is supposed to provide the required equipment, pay for work-related phone bills and be liable for property and personal health in cases of home-based telecommuting.

Child care expenses can either increase or decrease with telecommuting. If the employee perceives telecommuting as an alternative to child care, then a reduction in day care costs will be expected. However, if the employee perceives it to be difficult to work and take care of children simultaneously, an increase in day care expenditures may actually be expected.

A reduction in transportation costs is to be expected for both home- and telework center-based telecommuting. However, if the employer currently provides any type of commuting subsidy, such as a parking space, a transit pass or mileage expenses, the expected reduction in commuting costs will not be so significant. The overall sensitivity of the employee to changes in costs depends on how much these changes affect her/his available income.

- *IMPACT ON INCOME*

Changes in income are due to differences between the wages paid to telecommuters and commuting employees. Employees are expected to be more willing to accept incurring in some telecommuting costs than to accept a salary reduction. It is also expected that a salary reduction will be a higher disincentive to telecommuting than a salary increase will be an incentive.

The employee evaluates the benefits that telecommuting will bring and chooses to adopt the program if it offers higher benefits than those yielded by the conventional commuting arrangement.

SUMMARY

In this chapter, a comprehensive analytical framework for the telecommuting adoption process, including both the employer's and the employee's perspective, is developed. This framework incorporates the distinctions proposed by previous research and expands various aspects of it. In particular, it:

- acknowledges the complexity of the employer's decision process by identifying the various attributes that constitute a telecommuting program and characterizes the offering decision as the process of matching telecommuting arrangements and the employer's motivations, assessing the impacts of different arrangements on productivity, costs and managerial capabilities, and making an informed decision as to whether to make telecommuting available;

- defines the employee's decision to adopt telecommuting as a function not only of motivations, constraints and telecommuting costs, but also of the expected impact of telecommuting on the employee's lifestyle quality. Specifically, it is assumed that telecommuting adoption requires that the proposed arrangement actually address the employee's motivations in considering telecommuting.

This framework not only allows for the assessment of the potential of telecommuting to reduce work trips, but also provides a powerful tool for employers and employees to assess the potential of different arrangements to address their own questions regarding telecommuting.

The next stage involves designing a survey instrument to collect data with which to implement the proposed framework.

IV

A Survey of Telecommuting Preferences

Taking the above framework as a basis, a survey instrument is designed to collect the data used in the estimation of the model system that represents the telecommuting adoption process. In this chapter, the survey design is discussed and descriptive statistics of the data are presented.

THE SURVEY

Two different questionnaires are designed to collect data on the employer's and the employee's perceptions, attitudes and behavior regarding telecommuting. Each one of these questionnaires is discussed below.

The Employer's Survey

The employer's survey is designed to mirror the employer's decision process as described in the analytical framework. Its objective is to collect data with which to estimate a model of the decision to offer a telecommuting program as a function of the employer's motivations and constraints, as well as of the telecommuting attributes. The survey, presented in Appendix A, is divided into four main parts.

The first part — *Your experience with telecommuting* — asks questions about the employer's awareness of and experience with telecommuting arrangements, about the availability of a telecommuting program for the employees she/he supervises, and about possible motivations she/he would have to implement a program.

The second part — *The employees you supervise* — gathers information about the working structure of the group subordinated to the respondent. In particular, it inquires about the number of employees and contractors the employer supervises, and asks whether these employees work mostly in teams, mostly performing individual tasks, within a team structure, or mostly on individual projects.

The third part — *Your telecommuting program* — guides the respondent through the design and evaluation of a telecommuting program which would best suit the group she/he supervises. In this task, the employer is presented with a list of all the values of the attributes that constitute a telecommuting program, as indicated in Table 4.1, and asked to select the combination that best addresses her/his needs. She/he is also required to estimate the percentage change in employees' salary under telecommuting, if any. This *menu* approach constitutes a more realistic task than a choice from a reduced number of telecommuting programs generated by a factorial experimental design, since it allows the respondent to consider the complete set of alternatives which would be available for her/him to choose from if actually designing a program.

The employer is asked to design a program for her/his employees grouped in five different occupation categories: managerial, professional, administrative support, sales and other. If she/he currently offers a program to her/his employees, she/he is asked to refer to that program. She/he is also provided with one of three values of daily per capita rate ($150, $250 or $350) for the use of a telework center which provides basic office equipment and support, as well as access to a computer network.

She/he is then asked to assess the expected impact of the designed program on productivity, costs and on the organization overall. Specifically, she/he is asked to estimate the expected percentage change in employee direct costs, employee turnover costs and overhead. She/he is presented with a set of questions designed to measure the impact of telecommuting on the telecommuter's and on the telecommuter's group's productivity, as well as on managerial capabilities, on a scale from one (extremely negative) to nine (extremely positive). She/he is also required to assess the expected percentage change in productivity. Finally, she/he is asked if she/he would actually offer the designed program to her/his employees.

Table 4.1 Attributes of a Telecommuting Program

Attribute Description	Attribute Values
Minimum telecommuting days/week	0,1,2,3,4,5
Maximum telecommuting days/week	1,2,3,4,5
Flexibility of telecommuting schedule	fixed, flexible
Office space for commuting days	individual office, shared office, shared desk
Telecommuter's salary	lower, same, higher
Telecommuting space	home, telework center, either
Equipment required	computer, fax, computer network, dedicated phone line
Equipment provider	employer, employee
Responsibility for phone bills	employer, employee
Health and equipment liability	employer, employee

The fourth part — *About the organization you work for* — asks for information about the organization which may have an impact on the decision to offer telecommuting. In particular, these questions seek to identify whether the organization faces issues such as global competition and/or high costs of location in large urban areas, or whether the organization is going through some transition in structure and/or scale which may prompt the consideration of telecommuting. Finally, it looks for information such as size and industry, which can differentiate groups of organizations.

The Employee's Survey

The employee's survey is designed to guide the respondent through the adoption decision process, to collect data for the modeling stage, and to be compatible with the employer's decision process models. The survey, presented in Appendix B, is divided into four parts.

The first part — *Your telecommuting program* — inquires about the suitability of the respondent's job for telecommuting, the availability of a program which she/he can currently join, the characteristics of this program if available, and the respondent's motivations to adopting telecommuting.

The second part — *Your working week* — seeks to identify aspects of the respondent's job and commuting trip which can favor or constrain the adoption of telecommuting. It asks questions about the allocation of the employee's working hours to team work, interactions with customers and individual tasks, and regarding commuting frequency, commuting time and cost, and transportation mode.

The third part — *Choosing to adopt telecommuting* — is a stated preference experiment to identify the respondent's preferences for various telecommuting arrangements. Initially, the respondent is presented with three telecommuting scenarios created by a fractional factorial experimental design: one comparing two home-based telecommuting programs, one comparing two telework center-based telecommuting programs, and one comparing a home-based with a telework center-based telecommuting program.

The respondent is asked to choose her/his preferred arrangement in each pair, and to evaluate the potential impact of the chosen arrangement on her/his lifestyle and work-related costs. In particular, she/he is asked to assess the expected percentage change in her/his expenditure on child care, elder care, home utilities and overall working costs. She/he is also presented with a series of questions related to family and social life, productivity, career and job satisfaction, designed to measure the overall impact of a telecommuting arrangement on lifestyle, in a scale from one (extremely negative) to nine (extremely positive). Finally, she/he is requested to decide whether or not to adopt the chosen program, if offered.

The attributes that characterize each scenario are those presented in Table 4.1. Whenever a telework center-based program is presented, it is assumed that the employer provides the required equipment, pays for the work-related phone bills and assumes all the pertinent liabilities. The total number of scenarios is restricted by the fractional factorial design, but it is observed that all attribute levels are represented.

The eighteen different scenarios generated constitute six different surveys.

In the next stage, the respondent is guided through an additional task, using a *menu* approach. In this task, a list of all the values of the attributes that constitute a telecommuting program is presented, and the respondent is asked to design her/his ideal telecommuting arrangement. Then, she/he is asked about the expected impact of this program on her/his lifestyle and work-related costs in the same manner as described above. Finally, she/he is asked if she/he would actually adopt the designed program if it was offered by her/his employer.

The fourth part of the survey — *Personal information* — gathers personal data about the respondent, as well as data about the organization she/he works for, her/his job and her/his household. Organization-related questions include the industry the organization belongs to, whether the organization is undergoing any change in structure and/or scale, the office location and the type of commuting subsidies available to the employees. Job-related questions include type of occupation, employment status and time working for the company.

Individual- and household-related questions include gender, age, level of education, marital status, spouse's employment status, household income, number of persons and of children under six years of age in the household, number of children in day care, number of elder persons in the household requiring special care, house location, drivers' license and automobile availability for commuting, and type of information technology available in the household.

Innovative Features of the Survey

The survey instrument presented here has several innovative features. It recognizes and addresses the complexity of the telecommuting adoption process by:

- incorporating both the employer's and the employee's perspective;

- treating telecommuting as a combination of various attributes, each of which can assume various levels;

- distinguishing between respondents' preferences and choices, thus recognizing the relevance of situational constraints to the decision process;

- directly addressing the multifaceted aspects of productivity, costs and managerial capabilities, which are an organization's major concerns;

- directly addressing the various aspects of an employee's lifestyle and working costs that can be affected by telecommuting;

Moreover, compatibility between the employer's and the employee's data sets is assured, allowing for the integration of the two model systems. As such, this survey constitutes a powerful instrument for providing the required information for the understanding and modeling of the overall adoption process. Moreover, it presents the respondents with realistic choice contexts. It guides the respondents through a sequence of steps that mirror their decision processes. Thus, it not only allows for relevant data to be collected for the estimation of the proposed framework, but also constitutes a tool for providing both the employer and the employee with pertinent information and useful guidelines with which to assess the feasibility and desirability of telecommuting to address their needs.

THE DATA

The survey was distributed to a convenience sample of 120 organizations across the US in the industries of banking, finance, real estate, business services, government, consulting, education, telecommunications, computer hardware and software, and transportation. These industries were selected because their characteristics favor the implementation of telecommuting, and because organizations in these fields have actually implemented telecommuting programs (U.S.D.O.T. [13] and International Labour Organization [26]).

The organizations were selected from various mailing lists and were invited to participate by mail, phone calls or through personal contact with employees. Some surveys were mailed and some were transmitted through electronic mail. In general, the surveys that were mailed were all sent together to one person in the organization for distribution to the managers and employees. Therefore, no information is available about how many individuals actually received a copy of the survey and the response rate cannot be calculated.

For an organization to participate in the study, it was required that telecommuting be feasible for at least some of its employees. It was not required that a program be in place when the survey was administered. The employers' survey was distributed to individuals in managerial positions, supervising employees whose jobs could be performed with telecommuting. The employees' survey was distributed to individuals whose job could be performed at least partially with telecommuting.

The Employer's Data

Eighty managers from 28 different organizations responded. Nine percent of the respondents had no information about telecommuting prior to the survey. Some 51% knew about telecommuting from reading and 33% from another organization with which they had contact. About 49% had experienced telecommuting in their own organization and 54% were offering a telecommuting program to their employees at the time they answered the survey. These statistics indicate a high level in the sample of awareness of and experience with telecommuting.

Seventy-six percent of the respondents who completed the employers' survey supervise salaried employees who work primarily on individual tasks within a team structure, indicating no major structural constraint to the implementation of telecommuting. Seventy-seven percent worked out of the organization's headquarters, 9% out of a divisional branch and 10% out of a support services office.

The employers' survey does not contain any direct question about traffic congestion in the vicinity of the organization's office. A congestion variable is then constructed based on the total annual vehicle-miles traveled per mile of road in the state, and the population density for both the state and the city where each organization is located (US DOC [11] and Documents Index [14]). Those cities for which the total vehicle-miles traveled per mile of road was above 25 million are considered to be facing a high level of congestion. Based on this constructed variable, it is estimated that about 15% of the organizations are located in an area with heavily congested traffic.

About 21% of the organizations serve a local market, while 51% serve an international market, indicating a possible influence of the pressures due to the globalization of the economy on the telecommuting offering decision. About 33% of the businesses are related to computer software and hardware, 13% are consultants, 9% belong to the banking and finance industry, and 9% are governmental agencies.

All the employers supervise employees in managerial, professional or administrative support positions. None of them supervise employees in sales or other positions. On average, 27% of the supervised employees occupy managerial positions, 55% are professionals and 18% work in administrative support. Sixty-eight percent of the organizations are undergoing some structural or scale change. About 26% are expanding and 34% are reducing scale, 52% are undergoing a re-engineering process and 18% are relocating.

According to the literature, changes in the characteristics of the labor force are leading to a significant increase in the demand for flexible working arrangements (Kugelmass [31]). Such a trend is hinted at in the sample. About 65% of the respondents supervise employees who have demonstrated interest in telecommuting. About 41% of the respondents supervise employees who have formally requested permission to telecommute. Thus, employers would consider offering a telecommuting program primarily to address employees' personal needs, to attract other qualified employees and to increase individual productivity.

The data also indicates that cost reduction is not a major motivation for the respondents to offer telecommuting. Furthermore, there is more consistency around the concept of telecommuting as a tool to address productivity issues than to address cost issues. These results are summarized in Table 4.2.

To further develop the analysis, the sample is stratified into six segments, according to whether telecommuting is being considered for managers, professionals or administrative support staff, and whether the organization is located in a heavily congested area or not.

Observing the motivations of each of these groups, summarized in Table 4.3, some interesting differences are noted. For example, there seems to be a high level of consensus among employers of administrative support staff in congested areas about the possibility of adopting telecommuting to reduce labor costs and overhead. The same level of consensus or motivation is not observed for the other groups of employers. Employers supervising managers in organizations located in highly congested areas are generally more motivated to offer telecommuting than their counterparts in organizations located in non-congested areas. Employers of professionals in congested areas are mostly motivated by the need to address employees' personal needs, while there is more diversity on the motivations that lead employers of professionals in non-congested areas to consider telecommuting.

Table 4.2 Employer's Motivations for Offering Telecommuting

Variable Description (*)	mean	stdev
To address their personal needs	7.84	1.27
To attract skilled employees	6.52	1.88
To increase productivity	6.40	2.09
To reduce labor costs	5.53	2.64
To reduce/avoid overhead expenses	4.84	2.56

(*)Why would you offer telecommuting to your employees?
measured in a scale from 1, "definitely no" to 9, "definitely yes"

All employers are primarily motivated by the need to address employees' needs, as expected. Employers from congested areas are also very motivated by the need to increase productivity, while employers from non-congested areas are more motivated by the potential to attract new skilled employees.

These motivations are reflected in the resulting programs. When designing telecommuting arrangements for their employees, respondents tend to favor a flexible structure in which the concern for the employees' needs and productivity is the priority. As a general rule, respondents tend not to establish a minimum number of days in which telecommuting is required. On average, they limit the maximum telecommuting frequency to three days per week. They are unlikely to offer employees a shared desk to work at on commuting days. Salaries are likely to be kept the same for telecommuters and regular office workers.

Home-based arrangements are preferred to telework center-based ones. Not a single respondent designed an exclusively telework center-based arrangement. The basic technology required for home-based telecommuting consists of a computer and the connection to a

Table 4.3 Employer's Motivations to Offer a Telecommuting Program by Population Strata

Variable Description (*)	managers		professionals		admn. support	
	mean	stdev	mean	stdev	mean	stdev
Congested Areas						
To address their personal needs	8.25	0.96	8.43	0.79	8.75	0.50
To attract skilled employees	6.50	1.00	5.86	1.57	6.25	1.50
To increase productivity	7.50	1.73	6.57	2.76	7.75	1.89
To reduce labor costs	6.75	3.30	5.14	3.29	7.75	1.89
To reduce/avoid overhead expenses	4.75	3.10	4.00	2.65	6.50	1.91
Non Congested Areas						
To address their personal needs	7.88	1.03	7.62	1.54	7.82	1.01
To attract skilled employees	6.25	1.96	6.69	1.96	6.76	2.08
To increase productivity	6.17	1.93	6.24	2.23	6.47	1.84
To reduce labor costs	4.79	2.64	5.38	2.66	6.35	2.12
To reduce/avoid overhead expenses	4.33	2.58	4.71	2.61	5.88	2.29

(*) Why would you offer telecommuting to your employees?
measured in a scale from 1, "definitely no" to 9, "definitely yes"

computer network. Respondents are likely to propose that the employer provide the equipment and pay for installation and user costs.

Overall, respondents expect an increase in employee job satisfaction and an improvement in the quality of the work produced by telecommuters. No significant changes are expected in group productivity, team spirit and in the employer's ability to monitor employees. These results are summarized in Table 4.4.

Table 4.4 Expected Change in Productivity

Variable Description (*)	mean	stdev
Job satisfaction	7.57	1.13
Quality of telecommuter's work	6.33	1.58
Ability to attract qualified employees	6.65	1.61
Team spirit	5.20	1.81
Quality of team work	5.54	1.51
Ability to manage telecommuters	4.89	1.83
Ability to evaluate telecommuters	5.03	1.56

(*)What impact would you expect telecommuting to have on:
measured in a scale from 1, "extremely negative" to 9, "extremely positive"

The same segments described above are used to assess differences in the expected changes in productivity. The results are presented in Table 4.5. It can be observed that employers located in congested areas have a tendency to expect higher benefits from offering telecommuting to employees in managerial positions than employers located in non-congested areas do. The increase in job satisfaction is expected to be much higher for administrative support staff working in congested areas than for other employees. In general, there are no significant differences in the perceptions by employers of the impact on each group of employees for organizations located in non-congested areas. Employers from both areas expect the most significant impacts of telecommuting arrangements to be on job satisfaction and on the ability to attract qualified employees.

Employers from non-congested areas also expect a significant enhancement of the quality of professionals and administrative support staff work. Employers from congested areas see the potential for improvement in the quality of managers' work.

Table 4.5 Expected Change in Productivity by Population Strata

Variable Description (*)	managers		professionals		adm. support	
	mean	stdev	mean	stdev	mean	stdev
Congested Areas						
Job satisfaction	7.75	0.96	7.57	1.27	8.25	0.96
Quality of telecommuter's work	7.00	1.41	5.86	1.57	5.75	1.50
Ability to attract qualified employees	7.25	0.96	7.00	1.53	7.75	1.26
Team spirit	6.00	2.58	5.00	2.52	5.00	2.83
Quality of team work	6.50	1.91	5.86	1.21	5.75	1.50
Ability to manage telecommuters	6.25	1.50	5.57	1.81	5.50	1.73
Ability to evaluate telecommuters	6.00	1.83	5.29	1.70	6.25	1.50
Non Congested Areas						
Job satisfaction	7.33	1.05	7.51	1.11	7.59	1.37
Quality of telecommuter's work	6.46	1.44	6.22	1.55	6.71	1.76
Ability to attract qualified employees	6.46	1.35	6.67	1.35	6.59	1.80
Team spirit	5.08	1.47	5.24	1.49	5.35	2.23
Quality of team work	5.54	1.32	5.24	1.40	5.71	1.93
Ability to manage telecommuters	4.67	1.66	4.53	1.72	5.47	2.21
Ability to evaluate telecommuters	5.00	1.59	4.80	1.38	5.18	1.70

(*) What impact would you expect telecommuting to have on:

measured in a scale from 1 = extremely negative to 9 = extremely positive

Employee direct costs are expected to increase, employee turnover costs are expected to remain the same and overhead costs are expected to decrease due to the implementation of a telecommuting program. An overall positive impact on the organization is expected.

The Employee's Data

One hundred and seventy-six employees from 21 different organizations completed the employees' survey. About 40% of the respondents had a telecommuting program available, and about 32% were telecommuters at the time the survey was completed. About 67% of the respondents are professionals, while 15% have a managerial position and 15% work on administrative support tasks. The average respondent is a full-time salaried employee and works 5 days per week, out of which 4.3 days are spent in the organization's office and 0.7 days are spent working at home during business hours.

The average respondent works 8 hours per day in the organization's office, out of which 21.3% are spent on face-to-face interactions with customers or coworkers. She/he commutes an average of 35 minutes one way, primarily by car.

The average respondent is married, without children, member of a dual income household, about 39 years old, earning an individual annual income between 40,000 and 60,000 before taxes, and with an annual household income between 60,000 and 80,000 before taxes. About 59% of the respondents are females. More than half of the sample have completed a graduate program. About 18% have young children in day care and virtually nobody has elder individuals in the household requiring special care.

The average employee would telecommute primarily to have more flexibility. The desire to be more productive comes next in the order of motivations. The need to spend more time with the family and to have more job autonomy do provide some motivation and so do child care costs, whenever relevant. These results are summarized in Table 4.6.

When designing their ideal telecommuting program, respondents are unlikely to establish a minimum telecommuting frequency. On average, they allow a maximum of 4.7 telecommuting days a week and are likely to choose a flexible telecommuting schedule. They are likely to prefer home-based telecommuting and an individual office to work in commuting days. They would telecommute for the same salary that they are paid as regular commuters and they would like to have access to a computer and a computer network. A dedicated phone line and a fax machine are also desirable, but not a primary need. They would prefer the employer to provide the required equipment, to pay for work-related phone bills and to be liable for health and property insurance in cases of home-based telecommuting.

Table 4.6 Employee's Motivations to Adopt Telecommuting

Variable Description(*)	mean	stdev
Spend time with family	5.47	3.07
Be more productive	6.98	2.30
Have more flexibility	7.87	1.70
Have more job autonomy	5.34	2.43
Reduce child care costs	6.99	2.91

(*)Why would you telecommute?
  measured in a scale from 1, "definitely not" to 9, "definitely yes"

Respondents expect this ideal telecommuting program to have an overall positive impact on their lifestyle, affecting primarily their schedule flexibility. Job security and opportunity for promotion are barely affected. However, an increase in job autonomy and in individual and group productivity is expected, resulting in an overall increase in job satisfaction. Overall, life quality is expected to improve. These results are presented in Table 4.7.

In general, respondents did not assess the expected percentual change in work-related costs, only indicating whether they expected such costs to increase, decrease or remain the same. Respondents expected telecommuting to reduce both child care and overall working costs. Expenditures on home utilities were expected to increase with home telecommuting.

Assessment of the Data

The data set gathered for this study constitutes a unique source of information for the understanding of the telecommuting adoption process. Even though the number of observations in the employer's data set is rather limited, limiting the complexity of the models that can be estimated, it is a fairly diversified sample, allowing for the estimation of the impact of different organizational characteristics on the attitudes, preferences and choices with regard to telecommuting. The employee data set is much larger, allowing for more flexibility in the estimation stage. Both revealed and stated preference data are collected, allowing for the comparison between preferences and choices, and potential identification of some significant situational constraints.

Table 4.7 Expected Change in Lifestyle Quality

Variable Description (*):	mean	stdev
Your schedule flexibility	7.03	1.76
Your productivity	6.80	1.70
Your autonomy in your job	6.57	1.56
The productivity of the group you work with	5.60	1.63
Your family life	6.59	1.61
Your social life	5.80	1.69
Your job security	4.87	1.55
Your opportunity for promotion	4.61	1.57
Your sense of well being	6.81	1.75
Your job satisfaction	6.83	1.78
Your life, overall	6.81	1.70

(*)What impact do you expect telecommuting to have on:
measured in a scale from 1, " extremely negative" to 9, "extremely positive"

As far as the descriptive statistics are concerned, the data seem to fairly reflect the main issues regarding telecommuting presented in the literature. In particular, the employer's desire to address employees' needs is reflected in the program design, and a major demand from the employees for more flexibility is present in both data sets.

CONCLUSION

In this chapter, the design of the survey instrument to collect the data to model the adoption decision process is discussed and descriptive statistics of the sample are presented.

The survey takes a very comprehensive approach to telecommuting, and guides the respondents through all the necessary considerations to decide whether telecommuting is a desirable option to meet their needs. A rich data set is collected, providing the opportunity for the development of a comprehensive model system of the adoption process. The development of such model system is the objective of the next chapter.

V

Model System Estimation Results

In this chapter, the model system that represents the process of adoption of telecommuting is specified and estimated.

MODEL SYSTEM SPECIFICATION

The formulation of the model system that represents the adoption process is presented in this section. The models for the employer's and the employee's decision processes are presented separately.

The Employer's Model

The modeling framework for the employer's decision process is presented in Figure 5.1. This framework consists of two parts: the design of the telecommuting program and the decision to offer the designed program to the employees.

- *PROGRAM DESIGN*

In this first stage, the employer selects, from all possible telecommuting programs, the ones that can address her/his motivations, while satisfying existing constraints. In the framework

Telecommuting: The Decision Process

Figure 5.1 - The Employer's Decision Process - Modeling Framework

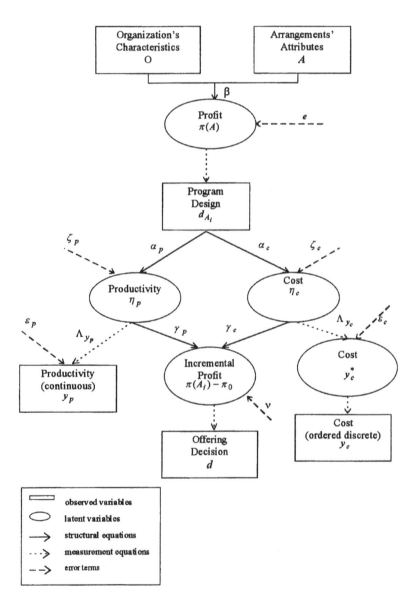

discussed in Chapter 3 it is assumed that the employer's objective is to maximize profit. In that same chapter, telecommuting is defined as a combination of attributes, each of which can assume various levels.

Given these assumptions, when designing a telecommuting program, the employer is searching for the combination of attribute values A_i that maximizes:

$$\pi(A_j) = Pf(A_j) - c(A_j), \quad A_j \in A, \quad A = \{A_1, \ldots, A_j, \ldots A_J\} \quad (5.1)$$

where A is the set of all possible combinations of the values of the attributes of a telecommuting program, A_j is the vector of attribute values that characterize program j, P is the price of the organization's product, and $\pi, f,$ and c are, respectively, the profit, the production and the cost functions of the organization.

To model the employer's choice of a program design, a probabilistic approach is adopted to account for the randomness due to lack of information about the organization's production function and cost structure, as well as for other unobserved factors. The following model is specified:

Structural Model:

$$\pi(A_i) = \beta_A A_i + \beta_W(W) + e_{A_i}, \quad A_i \in A \quad (5.2)$$

Measurement Model:

$$d_{A_i} = \begin{cases} 1, & if \ \pi(A_i) \geq \max_{A_j \in A} \pi(A_j) \\ 0, & otherwise \end{cases} \quad (5.3)$$

where:

A_i = $(K_A \times 1)$ vector of attribute values of telecommuting program i.

W = $(K_W \times 1)$ vector of interactions between telecommuting attributes and organization characteristics.

β_A = *(1x K_A)* vector of structural parameters.

β_W = *(1x K_W)* vector of structural parameters.

e_{A_i} = vector of random disturbance, distributed iid Gumbel (0,1).

A = set of all the telecommuting programs available to the employer.

d_A = *(1xA)* vector of dummy variables indicating the chosen telecommuting program.

The subscript relating to the individual respondent is omitted for simplicity. Given this specification, the likelihood of observing the vector of choices d_A, for a particular employer, given the set of all possible arrangements A and the organization characteristics O, can be written as:

$$L(d_A|A,O;\beta) = \prod_{A_i \in A} \left(\frac{e^{(\beta_A A_i + \beta_W W)}}{\sum_{A_j \in A} e^{(\beta_A A_j + \beta_W W)}} \right)^{d_{A_i}} \qquad (5.4)$$

where β is the set of structural parameters $\{\beta_A, \beta_W\}$. The estimation of these unknown parameter is performed by maximizing the logarithm of this likelihood function over the whole sample. In practice, the outcome of the employer's choice could be one or more telecommuting arrangements. For simplicity of the data collection process, it is assumed in this research that only one program is designed.

● *PROGRAM OFFERING DECISION*

In the next stage of the decision process, the employer compares the benefits and costs of the designed program with those of the currently available arrangement and decides whether to offer telecommuting to her/his employees. Let A_i denote the designed telecommuting program. The employer will offer it to her/his employees if:

$\pi(A_i) - \pi_0 > 0$, $\qquad (5.5)$

where $\pi(A_i)$ is the expected profit under the designed telecommuting arrangement and π_0 is the profit under the currently available arrangement.

As explained in Chapter 3, under the assumption that both prices and the total number of employees in the organization remain constant under both arrangements, the employer's decision is a function of expected changes in productivity and costs due to the implementation of the telecommuting program. These changes are influenced by the characteristics of the designed arrangement and constrained by the characteristics of the organization.

As discussed in Chapter 3, directly measuring changes in productivity and cost can be a difficult task. Thus, these changes are characterized by two latent variables, η_p and η_c, respectively. The *change in productivity* latent variable is measured by the employer's responses to the questions presented in Tables 4.4. These questions are measured in a nine points bipolar Likert scale, which favors the specification of a standard linear latent variable model (see Bollen [5] for details on latent variable models).

The *change in cost* latent variable is measured by the employer's responses to expected changes in employee direct costs, employee turnover costs and overhead. The responses to these questions posit a problem for the specification of a linear latent variable model. As explained in Chapter 4, the employer's survey required the respondents to estimate the expected percent change in these components of the organization's costs due to telecommuting. Such a response format would allow for the estimation of a linear latent variable model for the expected change in cost variable. However, the respondents only indicated whether they expected costs to increase, decrease or remain the same. As such, only discrete indicators of the latent cost variable are available, requiring the specification of a latent variable model with discrete ordered categorical indicators to estimate the expected changes in costs (see Gopinath [18] for details on this class of models).

Therefore, the employer's decision to offer the designed telecommuting program to her/his employees is modeled as a combination of a discrete choice model and latent variable models with continuous and discrete ordered categorical latent variables. The following specification is used:

Structural Model:

$$\eta_p = \alpha_{p_A} A_i + \alpha_{p_O} O + \alpha_{p_W} W + \zeta_p$$
$$\eta_c = \alpha_{c_A} A_i + \alpha_{c_O} O + \alpha_{c_W} W + \zeta_c \qquad\qquad (5.6)$$
$$\pi(A_i) - \pi_0 = \gamma_T + \gamma_p \eta_p + \gamma_c \eta_c + \gamma_O O + \nu$$

Measurement Model:

$$y_{pt} = \lambda_{y_{pt}} \eta_p + \lambda_{O_{pt}} O + \varepsilon_{pt} \qquad t = 1,...,T$$
$$y_{cq}^* = \lambda_{y_{cq}} \eta_c + \lambda_{O_{cq}} O + \varepsilon_{cq} \qquad q = 1,...,Q$$

$$y_{cq,m} = \begin{cases} 1, & if \ \tau_{cq,m-1} < y_{cq}^* \leq \tau_{cq,m} & q = 1,...,Q; \\ 0, & otherwise & m = 1,...,M \end{cases} \qquad (5.7)$$

$$d = \begin{cases} 1, & if \ \pi(A_i) - \pi_0 > 0 \\ 0, & if \ \pi(A_i) - \pi_0 \leq 0 \end{cases}$$

where:

η_p = latent change in productivity.

η_c = latent change in costs.

$\pi(A_i)$ = profit under the telecommuting arrangement.

π_0 = profit under the current working arrangement.

A_i = $(K_A x1)$ vector of arrangement attributes.

O = $(K_O x1)$ vector of organization's characteristics.

W = $(K_W x1)$ vector of interactions between arrangement attributes and organization's characteristics.

y_p = $(Tx1)$ vector of indicators of latent change in productivity.

y_c^* = $(Qx1)$ vector of latent indicators of latent change in costs.

y_c = (QxM) vector of observed indicators of latent change in costs.

d $\qquad$ = an indicator of the employer's decision.

α_{p_A} $\qquad$ = $(1 \times K_A)$ vector of structural parameters.

α_{p_O} $\qquad$ = $(1 \times K_O)$ vector of structural parameters.

α_{p_W} $\qquad$ = $(1 \times K_W)$ vector of structural parameters.

α_{c_A} $\qquad$ = $(1 \times K_A)$ vector of structural parameters.

α_{c_O} $\qquad$ = $(1 \times K_O)$ vector of structural parameters.

α_{c_W} $\qquad$ = $(1 \times K_W)$ vector of structural parameters.

γ $\qquad$ = $(1 \times (K_O + 3))$ vector of structural parameters.

λ_{y_p} $\qquad$ = $(T \times 1)$ vector of measurement parameters.

Λ_{O_p} $\qquad$ = $(T \times K_O)$ matrix of bias measurement parameters.

λ_{y_c} $\qquad$ = $(Q \times 1)$ vector of measurement parameters.

Λ_{O_c} $\qquad$ = $(Q \times K_O)$ matrix of bias measurement parameters.

τ $\qquad$ = $(Q \times (M+1))$ matrix of thresholds.
$\qquad$ The elements $\tau_{q,1} = -\infty$ and $\tau_{q,M+1} = +\infty$.

ζ_p $\qquad$ = a random term, distributed $N(0, \Psi_p)$.

ζ_c $\qquad$ = a random term, distributed $N(0,1)$.

v $\qquad$ = a random term, distributed iid Gumbel $(0,1)$.

ε_p $\qquad$ = $(T \times 1)$ vector of random terms, distributed $N(0, \Theta_p)$.

$\qquad$ Θ_p is a $(T \times T)$ diagonal variance matrix and $\theta_{p_{tt}}$ is its tth diagonal element.

ε_c $\qquad$ = $(Q \times 1)$ vector of random terms, distributed $N(0, I)$,

One of the elements of the λ_{y_p} vector is normalized to one for identification of the linear latent variable model. The normalization of the variance-covariance matrix of ε_c is required for identification of the latent variable model with discrete ordered categorical indicators, and to allow for the estimation of a different set of thresholds for each indicator of the latent variable. All error terms are assumed to be un-correlated with each other.

Given this specification, the joint likelihood of observing y_p , y_c, and d, given A_i and O, can be written as:

$$L(y_p, y_c, d | A_i, O; \gamma, \Lambda, \alpha, \tau, \Theta_p, \Psi_p) =$$

$$\int_{\eta_c} \int_{\eta_p} \left(\frac{1}{1 + e^{-\left(\gamma_T + \gamma_p \eta_p + \gamma_c \eta_c + \gamma_O O\right)}} \right)^d *$$

$$\left(1 - \frac{1}{1 + e^{-\left(\gamma_T + \gamma_p \eta_p + \gamma_c \eta_c + \gamma_O O\right)}} \right)^{(1-d)} *$$

$$\prod_{t=1}^{T} \frac{1}{(\theta_{P_{tt}})^{1/2}} \phi \left(\frac{y_{pt} - \lambda_{pt} \eta_p - \lambda_{O_{pt}} O)}{(\theta_{P_{tt}})^{1/2}} \right) *$$

$$\prod_{q=1}^{Q} \prod_{m=1}^{M} \left[\Phi(\tau_{cq,m} - \lambda_{y_{cq}} \eta_c - \lambda_{O_{cq}} O) - \right.$$

$$\left. \Phi(\tau_{cq,m-1} - \lambda_{y_{cq}} \eta_c - \lambda_{O_{cq}} O) \right]^{y_{cq,m}} *$$

$$\frac{1}{(\Psi_p)^{1/2}} \phi \left(\frac{\eta_p - \alpha_{p_A} A_i - \alpha_{p_O} O - \alpha_{p_W} W}{(\Psi_p)^{1/2}} \right) *$$

(5.8)

$$\phi(\eta_c - \alpha_{c_A} A_i - \alpha_{c_O} O - \alpha_{c_W} W) d\eta_p d\eta_c$$

where ϕ and Φ are respectively the probability density function and the cumulative distribution function of the standard normal distribution. The estimation process maximizes the logarithm of this likelihood function over the whole sample.

The Employee's Model

The model that explains the employee's decision to adopt telecommuting, given that a program is offered, consists of two parts: the program choice and the telecommuting adoption decision. The modeling framework is presented in Figures 5.2 and 5.3. Figure 5.2 shows the employee's telecommuting preference model. Figure 5.3 shows the telecommuting decision process, given these preferences. A discussion of this framework is presented below.

- **PROGRAM CHOICE**

As explained in Chapter 3, the employee is assumed to have a utility maximization behavior and to be driven by some particular motivation to adopt telecommuting. Therefore, when choosing a telecommuting program from among the options made available by the employer, the employee is searching for the combination of attribute values A_i that maximizes:

$$U = U(A_j), \quad A_j \in A, \; A = \{A_1, ..., A_j, ..., A_J\} \tag{5.9}$$

where A is the set of all possible arrangements, A_j is the vector of attribute values that characterize alternative j and U is the employee's utility function.

It is assumed that the employee has a preferred arrangement from the set of all possible arrangements. A telecommuting program from the constrained choice set she/he is offered by the employer is chosen if it is the closest to the preferred arrangement. Given these assumptions, the model that explains the employee's preferences, presented in Figure 5.2, is specified as follows:

Structural Model:

$$U_p(A_i) = \beta^p_A A_i + \beta^p_G G + e^p_{A_i}, \quad A_i \in A \tag{5.10}$$

Measurement Model:

$$d^p_{A_i} = \begin{cases} 1, & \text{if } U_p(A_i) \geq \max_{A_j \in A} U_p(A_j) \\ 0, & \text{otherwise} \end{cases} \tag{5.11}$$

Figure 5.2 - The Employee's Preferred Arrangement Model

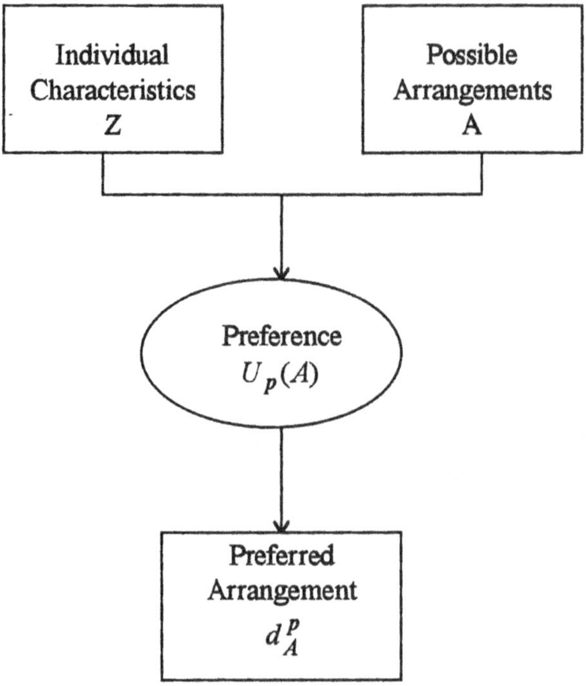

where:

U_p = *(Jx1)* vector of utilities derived from the arrangements in the unconstrained choice set.

A_i = *(K_Ax1)* vector of attribute values of telecommuting program i.

G = *(K_Gx1)* vector of interactions between the arrangement attributes and the employee characteristics.

β_A^P = *(1x K_A)* vector of structural parameters.

$\beta^P_G = (1x\,K_G)$ vector of structural parameters.

$e^P_A = (Jx1)$ vector of random terms, distributed iid Gumbel $(0,1)$.

A = set of all the telecommuting programs considered by the employee.

$d^P_A = (Jx1)$ vector of dummy variables indicating the employee's preferred program.

Given this specification, the likelihood of observing d^P_A, given A and Z, is given by:

$$L(d^P_A|A,Z;\beta)= \prod_{A_i\,\in A}\left(\frac{e^{(\beta_A A_i+\beta_G G)}}{\displaystyle\sum_{A_j\,\in A}e^{(\beta_A A_j+\beta_G G)}}\right)^{d_{A_i}} \qquad (5.12)$$

where $\beta=\{\beta_A,\beta_G\}$. The model parameters are estimated by maximizing the logarithm of this likelihood function over the whole sample.

The above model explains the employee's preference, given the set of all possible telecommuting arrangements. However, the telecommuting program offered by the employer does not include all the possible telecommuting arrangements, but only the ones which address the employer's motivations and constraints. Therefore, when choosing a telecommuting arrangement to consider for adoption, the employee selects an arrangement from the constrained choice set made available by the employer. This choice is based on the employee's preference and on the characteristics of the arrangements made available by the employer. Therefore, given the estimation results of the preference model and the set of arrangements offered by the employer, the employee's program choice model is specified as:

Figure 5.3 - The Employee's Decision Process - Modeling Framework

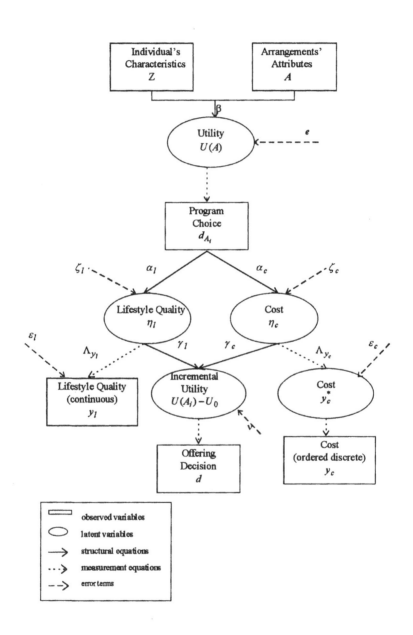

Structural Model:

$$U_C(A_i) = \beta^C U_p(A_i) + e^C_{A_i}, \quad A_i \in A_M \qquad (5.13)$$

Measurement Model:

$$d^C_{A_i} = \begin{cases} 1, & if \ \ U_C(A_i) \geq \max_{A_i \in A_M} U_C(A_i) \\ 0, & otherwise \end{cases} \qquad (5.14)$$

where:

U_p = *(Kx1)* vector of fitted utilities from the preferred
   arrangement model.
U_C = *(Kx1)* vector of utilities derived from arrangements in the
   constrained choice set.
β^C = a structural parameter.
e^C_A = *(Kx1)* vector of random terms, distributed iid Gumbel (0,1).
A_M = set of K telecommuting programs offered by the employer.
d^C_A = *(Kx1)* vector of dummy variable indicating the employee's
   chosen program.
The likelihood of observing d^C_A, given A_M and U_p, is given by:

$$L(d^C_A | A_M, U_p; \beta^C) = \prod_{A_j \in A_M} \left(\frac{e^{(\beta^C U_p(A_j))}}{\sum_{A_j \in A_M} e^{(\beta^C U_p(A_j))}} \right)^{d_{A_j}} \qquad (5.15)$$

- *PROGRAM ADOPTION DECISION*

Let A_i denote the telecommuting program the employee selects from the set offered by the employer. She/he will choose to adopt it if:

$$U(A_i) - U_0 > 0, \qquad\qquad (5.16)$$

where $U(A_i)$ is the expected utility under the selected telecommuting arrangement and U_0 is the utility under the current work arrangement. This decision is influenced by the characteristics of the arrangement, as well as by the individual's characteristics and situational constraints.

In Chapter 3, three major areas that affect the employee's decision to adopt telecommuting were identified: lifestyle quality, work-related costs and income. Changes in income are directly included in the telecommuting scenarios. Changes in lifestyle quality and work-related costs are defined as two latent variables, η_l and η_c, respectively. The *change in lifestyle quality* latent variable is measured by the employee's responses to the questions presented in Table 4.7.

The employee's responses to these questions are measured in a nine point bipolar Likert scale, which allows for the specification of a linear latent variable model.

The *change in work-related cost* variable is measured by the employee's responses to questions about the expected change in home office utility costs, child and elder care costs and overall working costs. As explained in Chapter 4, the employees were required to assess the percent change in these components of the work-related costs. However, most of these employees only indicated if costs were expected to increase, decrease or remain the same. As such, only discrete ordered categorical indicators are available for the expected change in working costs. The following model is thus specified to explain the employee's decision to adopt telecommuting:

Structural Model:

$$\eta_1 = \alpha_{1_A} A_i + \alpha_{1_Z} Z + \alpha_{1_G} G + \zeta_1$$

$$\eta_c = \alpha_{c_A} A_i + \alpha_{c_Z} Z + \alpha_{c_G} G + \zeta_c \tag{5.17}$$

$$U(A_i) - U_0 = \gamma_0 + \gamma_1 \eta_1 + \gamma_c \eta_c + \gamma_A A_i + v$$

Measurement Model:

$$y_{lr} = \lambda_{y_{lr}} \eta_1 + \lambda_{Z_{lr}} Z + \varepsilon_{lr} \qquad\qquad r = 1, \ldots, R$$

$$y^*_{cq} = \lambda_{y_{cq}} \eta_c + \lambda_{Z_{cq}} Z + \varepsilon_{cq} \qquad\qquad q = 1, \ldots, Q$$

$$\tag{5.18}$$

$$y_{cq,m} = \begin{cases} 1, & \text{if } \tau_{cq,m-1} < y^*_{cq} \leq \tau_{cq,m} & q = 1, \ldots, Q \\ 0, & \text{otherwise} & m = 1, \ldots, M \end{cases}$$

$$d = \begin{cases} 1, & \text{if } U(A_i) - U_0 > 0 \\ 0, & \text{if } U(A_i) - U_0 \leq 0 \end{cases}$$

where:

η_1 = latent change in lifestyle quality.

η_c = latent change in work-related costs.

$U(A_i)$ = utility under the chosen telecommuting arrangement.

U_0 = utility under the commuting arrangement.

A_i = $(K_A x1)$ vector of arrangement attributes.

Z = $(K_Z x1)$ vector of the employee's characteristics.

G = $(K_G x1)$ vector of interactions between the program attributes and the employee's characteristics.

y_l $\quad$ = *(Rx1)* vector of indicators of latent change in lifestyle quality.

y_c^* $\quad$ = *(Qx1)* vector of latent indicators of latent change in work-related costs.

y_c $\quad$ = *(QxM)* vector of indicators of latent change in work-related costs.

α_{l_A} $\quad$ = *(1x K_A)* vector of structural parameters.

α_{l_Z} $\quad$ = *(1x K_Z)* vector of structural parameters.

α_{l_G} $\quad$ = *(1x K_G)* vector of structural parameters.

α_{c_A} $\quad$ = *(1x K_A)* vector of structural parameters.

α_{c_Z} $\quad$ = *(1x K_Z)* vector of structural parameters.

α_{c_G} $\quad$ = *(1x K_G)* vector of structural parameters.

γ $\quad$ = *(1x $(3+K_A)$)* vector of structural parameters.

λ_{y_l} $\quad$ = *(Rx1)* vector of measurement parameters.

Λ_{Z_l} $\quad$ = *(Rx K_Z)* matrix of bias measurement parameters.

λ_{y_c} $\quad$ = *(Qx1)* vector of measurement parameters.

Λ_{Z_c} $\quad$ = *(Qx K_Z)* matrix of bias measurement parameters.

τ_c $\quad$ = *(Qx(M+1))* matrix of thresholds for changes in work-related costs. The elements $\tau_{cq,1=-\infty}$ and $\tau_{cq,M+1=+\infty}$

ζ_l $\quad$ = a random term, distributed $N(0,\Psi_l)$

ζ_c $\quad$ = a random term, distributed $N(0,1)$.

ε_l $\quad$ = *(Rx1)* vector of random terms, distributed $N(0,\Theta_l)$, Θ_l is a *(RxR)* diagonal variance matrix.

ε_c $\quad$ = *(Qx1)* vector of random terms, distributed $N(0,I)$.

ν $\quad$ = a random disturbance, distributed iid Gumbel (0,1).

One of the elements of λ_{y_l} is normalized to be the scale of the latent lifestyle quality model. The normalization of the variance-covariance matrix of ε_c is required for identification of the latent cost model. All the error terms are uncorrelated with each other.

The likelihood of observing y_l, y_c and d, given A_i and Z can then be written as:

$$L(y_l, y_c, d \mid A_i, Z; \gamma, \Lambda, \alpha, \tau, \Theta_l, \Psi_l) =$$

$$\int_{\eta_c} \int_{\eta_l} \left(\frac{1}{1 + e^{-(\gamma_0 + \gamma_l \eta_l + \gamma_c \eta_c + \gamma_A A_i)}} \right)^d *$$

$$\left(1 - \frac{1}{1 + e^{-(\gamma_0 + \gamma_l \eta_l + \gamma_c \eta_c + \gamma_A A_i)}} \right)^{(1-d)} *$$

$$\prod_{r=1}^{R} \frac{1}{(\theta_{l_{rr}})^{1/2}} \phi \left(\frac{y_{lr} - \lambda_{lr} \eta_l - \lambda_{Z_{lr}} Z}{(\theta_{l_{rr}})^{1/2}} \right) *$$

$$\prod_{q=1}^{Q} \prod_{m=1}^{M} \left[\Phi(\tau_{cq,m} - \lambda_{y_{cq}} \eta_c - \lambda_{Z_{cq}} Z) - \right.$$

$$\left. \Phi(\tau_{cq,m-1} - \lambda_{y_{cq}} \eta_c - \lambda_{Z_{cq}} Z) \right]^{y_{cqm}} *$$

$$\frac{1}{(\Psi_l)^{1/2}} \phi \left(\frac{\eta_l - \alpha_{p_A} A_i - \alpha_{p_Z} Z - \alpha_{p_G} G}{(\Psi_l)^{1/2}} \right) *$$

$$\phi(\eta_c - \alpha_{c_A} A_i - \alpha_{c_Z} Z - \alpha_{c_G} G) d\eta_l d\eta_c \tag{5.19}$$

where ϕ and Φ are respectively the probability density function and the cumulative distribution function of the standard normal distribution. The model estimation maximizes the logarithm of this likelihood function over the whole sample.

MODEL SYSTEM ESTIMATION

In this section the model estimation process is discussed and the final estimation results are presented. The employer's and the employee's model systems are analyzed separately.

The Employer's Model

As explained earlier in this chapter, the employer's decision process is modeled in two stages: program design and program offering decision. Each one of these stages is discussed in order.

- *PROGRAM DESIGN*

In the program design stage, the employer selects the combination of attribute values that best fits her/his motivations to consider telecommuting, given her/his situational constraints.

♦ *HYPOTHESES*

In the model specification, some hypotheses are made regarding differences in behavior due to organizational characteristics. First, it is assumed that if employees work primarily on a team structure, the employer would be less likely to require a minimum telecommuting frequency and would allow for fewer telecommuting days than if employees worked primarily on individual tasks. Moreover, employers from organizations adopting a team structure should place a higher value on schedule flexibility than employers from organizations adopting an individual task structure.

It is assumed that employers from organizations located in congested areas would be more likely to prefer arrangements in which a minimum telecommuting is required and allow for more telecommuting days than employers of organizations located in non-congested areas. Requiring a minimum frequency would help employers to deal with traffic congestion issues and possibly to address some office space problems. Allowing for many telecommuting days would address both of these issues and provide increased flexibility to employees to address their personal needs.

It is assumed that differences in behavior should be expected due to the organization's scale. Generically, a large organization is expected to be more rigid than a small one in terms of its organizational structure. Therefore, large organizations are expected to be more restrictive as far as the telecommuting frequency is concerned, and to prefer a fixed over a flexible schedule. Furthermore, large organizations are under government mandate to reduce traffic congestion, and if offering telecommuting, would tend to design a program that addresses this issue.

As far as the office space is concerned, it is hypothesized that an employer would be more likely to offer a shared desk for the employees to work at on commuting days if a higher telecommuting frequency is allowed. She/he would be more likely to offer reduced salary to administrative support staff, who are easier to replace, than to employees occupying professional or managerial positions. On the other hand, she/he would be more likely to provide equipment, pay bills and be liable for property and safety, if the program is being designed for administrative support staff. These employees are less likely to already have such equipment at home and the potential cost savings in office space from allowing them to telecommute would be significant enough to compensate for these expenditures.

♦ *SPECIFICATION ISSUES*

All the attributes that constitute a telecommuting program are included in the model specification, except for a variable indicating whether a computer is required. Even though the computer requirement is one of the attributes of the telecommuting arrangement, virtually all respondents chose to have a computer available. Therefore, all the arrangements for which a computer is not available are excluded from the employer's choice set, and the specified model does not include a computer availability variable. All the variables are dummies, except for the minimum and the maximum telecommuting days per week, which vary from zero or one to five, respectively.

As mentioned in Chapter 4, none of the respondents chose to design a telecommuting program which was exclusively telework center-based. About 80% of the respondents selected exclusively home-based telecommuting programs and some 20% of the respondents chose to make either option available for their employees to choose. As such, a dummy variable was created to indicate the programs in which the employee is given the option to choose between home- and telework center-based telecommuting.

As mentioned in Chapter 4, the choice set available for the respondents to choose from contained over 90,000 alternatives. Therefore, a random sample of alternatives is used for model estimation purposes. After some trials with different sample sizes, a sample of 60 arrangements, including the one selected by the employer, was chosen.

This sample size is large enough to indicate the significance of each of the attributes to the employer's choice, and not too large to cause significant computational problems.

◆   *ESTIMATION RESULTS*

The hypotheses described above are tested in various iterations of the model estimation. Initially, a simple model specification, including only the attributes that constitute a telecommuting program, was tried. The results of this initial model indicate that the average employer would prefer programs with a flexible telecommuting schedule, in which no minimum telecommuting frequency is required. Her/his preference for an arrangement would decrease as the maximum number of telecommuting days allowed increases.

The average employer would be unlikely to provide the employee with a shared desk to work at on commuting days, or to pay telecommuters a lower salary than they would be paid as regular commuters. Available access to a computer network is a major benefit. Availability of a fax machine and a dedicated phone line also increases the preference for a program, but not so drastically as the access to a computer network. The employer would be likely to provide all the required equipment, pay for all work-related phone bills an be liable for property and the employee's safety and health in home-based telecommuting programs.

The results of subsequent estimates indicate no significant differences in behavior between employers of organizations located in congested and non-congested areas, as far as the program design is concerned. Also, no significant behavioral differences are noticed between employers of individuals on professional or managerial occupations and employers of administrative support staff as far as salary payment, equipment provision and costs responsibilities are concerned. Furthermore, even though the likelihood of offering a shared desk for employees to work at on commuting days does increase as the maximum telecommuting frequency allowed increases, the difference is not significant.

However, the difference in behavior between employers of organizations adopting a team structure and those adopting an individual task structure, as far as establishing a minimum telecommuting frequency, is significant. While employers adopting a team structure tend not to require a minimum telecommuting frequency, the preference for a program by employers adopting an individual task structure increases as the minimum frequency increases. This difference may indicate that an individual task structure allows employers to benefit not only from the telecommuting potential to increase productivity, but also from its cost savings potential, since requiring a minimum frequency allows for some office space savings.

In order to test for behavioral differences due to an organization's scale, two separate models, for small and large organizations, were estimated. Large organizations herein are those in which the respondent of the survey supervises more than 50 employees. The results indicate that while small organizations tend to not establish a minimum telecommuting frequency at all, large organizations would prefer to establish a minimum telecommuting frequency if employees work primarily on individual tasks. While large organizations tend to prefer a fixed telecommuting schedule, small organizations prefer to have schedule flexibility. Large organizations would prefer not to have access to a computer network, while small organizations would strongly prefer to have access to a computer network. Large organizations are more likely to already have their own network, and access to an external network is not required. There are no significant differences as far as the preferences for the remaining attributes are concerned.

Given this analysis, the final model specification, presented in Table 5.1, is adopted to explain the design process. This specification highlights the significant differences in organization's behavior due to differences in scale and structure. In general, small organizations, or organizations with a team structure, tend to prefer more flexible arrangements than large organizations or organizations adopting an individual task structure.

- *PROGRAM OFFERING DECISION*

Once a telecommuting program is designed, the employer assesses its potential impact on productivity and costs, compares the expected benefits with those yielded by the current arrangement and chooses to offer telecommuting if it maximizes the organization's profit.

Table 5.1 Employer's Program Design

Variable Description	estimate	t-statistic
Minimum telecommuting days per week, team structure	-0.93	-27.48
Minimum telecommuting days per week, individual structure, large organizations	1.04	33.13
Minimum telecommuting days per week, individual structure, small organizations	-0.46	-41.05
Maximum telecommuting days per week	-0.18	-21.58
Flexible telecommuting schedule, large organizations	-0.58	-8.96
flexible telecommuting schedule, small organizations	1.07	43.30
Shared desk offered for commuting days	-1.71	-50.48
Lower salary paid to telecommuters	-2.37	-51.57
Telework center telecommuting	-1.21	-49.50
Fax machine required	0.52	23.52
Dedicated phone line required	0.59	27.02
Access to computer network required, large organizations	-0.89	-12.80
Access to computer network required, small organizations	2.02	61.75
Employer provides equipment	1.14	47.66
Employer pays phone bills	1.91	64.63
Employer is liable for property and safety	0.32	14.25
Number of observations	104	
Number of cases	6136	
Log-likelihood at zero	-425.8	
Log-likelihood at convergence	-249.1	
Adjusted rho-squared	0.4	

In the estimation process initially the productivity and the cost latent variable models were defined separately, and then a joint estimation of the latent variable models and the choice model was performed. A discussion of these three stages follows.

• *Telecommuting Impacts on Productivity*

♦ HYPOTHESES

It is assumed that telecommuting can lead to some increase in productivity by giving the employee flexibility to adjust her/his schedule to fit the work load and her/his personal needs. If this initial hypothesis is correct, establishing a minimum telecommuting frequency required should have a negative impact on productivity, while allowing for high telecommuting frequency and for a flexible telecommuting schedule should have a positive impact on productivity. The perceived impact of schedule flexibility on productivity, however, is expected to vary according to the organization's size.

A lower salary paid to telecommuters is expected to negatively affect productivity. A similar impact is expected if a telework center-based telecommuting program is offered. It is further hypothesized that employers located in highly congested areas perceive a higher potential for productivity improvement through telecommuting than employers located in non-congested areas. Finally, it is assumed that the potential for productivity improvements varies according to the characteristics of each industry.

It is assumed that each of the indicators vary differently, according to certain characteristics of the organization. In particular, it is assumed that if the organization currently offers a telecommuting program, the respondents tend to state a higher expected impact on all indicators of productivity than if a program were not available. If the employees in the organization have requested permission to telecommute, a higher impact on job satisfaction should be expected from offering a program than if the employees have demonstrated no interest. If an organization serves an international market, telecommuting is expected to have a higher impact on the ability to attract new, qualified employees than if the organization serves a local or regional market. In particular, consulting companies are hypothesized to expect a higher impact on job satisfaction and on the ability to attract qualified employees than other organizations. Employers in organizations adopting a team structure are hypothesized to expect a higher impact on individual productivity and a lower impact on team spirit and the quality of team work than employers in organizations adopting an individual task structure.

◆   *ESTIMATION RESULTS*

All these hypotheses were tested in various iterations of the model. In the measurement model, the expected impact on job satisfaction is normalized as the scale of the measurement model. The coefficients of the other indicators are allowed to vary freely. The results of the best specification are presented in Table 5.2.

It was verified that there are no significant differences in perception of the impact of telecommuting on productivity between organizations due to differences in scale, structure, industry or location. However, the differences in perception are significant between consulting companies and other organizations as regards job satisfaction and ability to attract qualified employees. The impacts of the arrangement characteristics on productivity is as expected.

●   *Telecommuting Impacts on Cost*

◆   *HYPOTHESES*

Telecommuting affects the organization's expenditures on office space, equipment, telecommunications, insurance, salaries and overheads. It is assumed that an employer should expect a reduction in cost if she/he offers the employee a shared desk to work at on commuting days, or a lower salary than she/he is currently paid. Costs should be expected to increase if the employer provides the required equipment, pays for work-related phone bills and has increased liability for property and employee safety.

If a telework center-based program is implemented, costs are expected to increase. If the organization is located in a congested area, telecommuting is expected to have a higher potential for cost savings than otherwise. In particular, higher savings should be expected as far as office space is concerned.

Table 5.2 - Telecommuting Impact on Productivity

Variable Description	estimate	t-statistic
Structural Model		
Minimum telecommuting required	-0.11	-3.55
Maximum telecommuting allowed	0.10	2.97
Lower salary to telecommuters	-0.29	-2.73
Telework center telecommuting	-0.12	-2.15
Measurement Model		
Employee's job satisfaction	1.00	--------
- Consulting company	0.57	2.81
Quality of telecommuters' work	2.84	4.05
Ability to attract qualified employees	2.12	3.70
- Consulting company	0.67	2.81
Team spirit	2.56	3.73
Quality of telecommuters' group work	2.81	4.03
Ability to manage telecommuters	3.61	4.06
Ability to evaluate telecommuters' perform-ance	2.99	4.06
Standard Deviation		
$\theta 1$ (employee's job satisfaction)	1.02	14.25
$\theta 2$ (quality of telecommuter's work)	0.93	12.46
$\theta 3$ (ability to attract qualified employees)	1.28	13.86
$\theta 4$ (team spirit)	1.39	13.74
$\theta 5$ (quality of telecommuter's group work)	0.85	12.47
$\theta 6$ (ability to manage telecommuters)	0.87	9.91
$\theta 7$ (ability to evaluate telecommuter's performance)	0.80	11.36
ψ (productivity latent variable)	0.45	4.13
Number of observations	105	
Squared multiple correlation of structural equation	0.11	
Log-likelihood at zero	-1584.3	
Log-likelihood at convergence	-1170.4	

♦ *ESTIMATION RESULTS*

These hypotheses were tested in various iterations of the model. The results indicate that the only arrangement characteristics that have a significant impact on an organization's costs are those related to the use of office space on commuting days and to the liability involved in home-based telecommuting. This may indicate that telecommuting is more likely to be adopted due to its potential to increase productivity than to reduce costs. The latter becomes relevant when the scale of telecommuting is large enough to allow for office space reduction.

Offering telecommuters a shared desk to work at on commuting days decreases costs, since it allows for office space savings. Offering telecommuters a lower salary, however, has a low potential for cost reduction. If the employer pays for the phone bills, an increase in costs is expected. Similarly, when the employer is liable for property and employee health under a home-based telecommuting arrangement, some additional expenditure is expected, since new types of insurance may be required.

The provision of equipment, which in this case refers primarily to a computer, does not have a significant impact on costs. Moreover, the sign of the corresponding coefficient is counter-intuitive. Therefore, the variable was excluded from the final specification. The cost impact of renting a telework center space was negligible. Therefore this variable is also removed from the final model. If the organization is located in an area of heavily congested traffic, the potential of telecommuting to reduce costs increases, as expected. The final specification is presented in Table 5.3.

• *Telecommuting Offering Decision*

♦ *HYPOTHESES*

Given the assumption that prices and number of employees under all working arrangements remain constant, the decision to offer a telecommuting program is a function of its impact on productivity and costs, as well as on the organization's characteristics and situational constraints.

In particular, an employer in an organization in which the employees have requested permission to telecommute is expected to perceive a higher benefit from telecommuting than other employers.

Table 5.3 - Telecommuting Impact on Costs

Variable Description	estimates	t-statistics
Structural Equation		
Shared desk available for commuting days	-2.012	-4.54
Reduced salary to telecommuters	-0.438	-0.80
Phone bills paid by employer	0.611	1.63
Liability costs paid by employer	0.740	2.60
Heavily congestion area	-0.750	-1.97
Measurement Equation		
Employee direct cost	0.911	4.03
Employee turnover cost	0.186	1.58
Overhead cost	2.287	1.49
Thresholds		
τ_{11} (employee direct cost)	-1.159	-4.86
τ_{12} (employee direct cost)	0.688	3.68
τ_{21} (employee turnover cost)	-0.372	-2.88
τ_{22} (employee turnover cost)	1.966	7.31
τ_{31} (employee overhead cost)	-2.112	-1.74
τ_{32} (employee overhead cost)	1.631	1.60
Number of observations	103	
Squared multiple correlation of the structural equation	0.39	
Log-likelihood at zero	-9710.4	
Log-likelihood at convergence	-257.5	

An employer who has some experience with telecommuting is expected to favor it more than employers with no previous experience. Finally, an employer whose organization is relocating is expected to derive less benefit from telecommuting than other employers, since relocation is supposed to be a substitute for telecommuting, as far as cost reduction policies are concerned.

♦ *ESTIMATION RESULTS*

Given these hypotheses, various iterations of the model were estimated. The results of the latent variable models are similar to those presented previously, and will not be discussed further. The choice model indicates that if an increase in productivity is expected, the probability of the arrangement being offered increases. If an increase in cost is expected, the probability of the arrangement being offered decreases. The employee's request to telecommute is a major motivation for adoption, and the lack of information about telecommuting is a major barrier. There is some potential endogeneity associated with the employee request- and the information-related variables, but the available data does not allow this hypothesis to be tested. Relocation functions as a substitute for telecommuting, as expected. The final results of the joint estimation procedure are presented in Table 5.4.

The Employee's Model

The employee's decision process is modeled in two parts: program choice and program adoption decision. Each of these parts is discussed separately.

- *PROGRAM CHOICE*

When offered more than one telecommuting arrangement by the employer, it is assumed that the employee will select the one that best addresses her/his needs and then decide whether or not to adopt it. It is assumed that the employee has in mind a preferred telecommuting arrangement, as explained previously. The probability of an employee choosing a program offered by the employer increases as her/his preference for the program increases.

- *PREFERRED PROGRAM MODEL*
It is hypothesized that single parents of young children or those whose spouses also have a paid job would be likely to place a higher value on flexibility than other employees. These individuals are also expected to be more averse to telework centers than others. It is also assumed that individuals with low income would be more sensitive to telecommuting costs and salary reduction then individuals in a high income level. Finally, differences in preferences for telecommuting frequency due to the structure of the organization are expected. In particular, employees working in a team structure are expected to derive more benefits from the possibility of working at home than employees working individu-

ally. For the former group, telecommuting would increase autonomy and avoid continuous interruptions to their work.

Table 5.4 - Telecommuting Offering Decision

Variable Description	estimate	t-statistic
Change in Productivity		
Structural Model		
Minimum telecommuting days allowed	-0.11	-3.49
Maximum telecommuting days required	0.10	2.94
Reduced salary paid to telecommuters	-0.29	-2.67
Telework center	-0. 11	-2.03
Measurement Model		
Employees' job satisfaction	1.00	------
- Consulting company	0.78	3.96
Quality of work produced by telecommuters	2.85	3.09
Ability to attract other qualified employees	2.13	3.64
- Consulting company	0.78	3.09
Team spirit among the group you supervise	2.58	3.63
Quality of work produced by the whole group	2.76	3.94
Ability to manage telecommuters	3.62	3.97
Ability to evaluate telecommuter performance	2.99	3.97
Standard Deviations		
θ_1 (employee's job satisfaction)	1.02	13.89
θ_2 (quality of telecommuters' work)	0.94	12.11
θ_3 (ability to attract qualified employees)	1.26	13.49
θ_4 (team spirit among group you supervise)	1.42	13.39
θ_5 (quality of group work)	0.83	12.01
θ_6 (ability to manage telecommuters)	0.89	9.66
θ_7 (ability to evaluate telecom. performance)	0.82	11.38
Ψ (productivity latent variable)	0.45	4.05
Squared multiple correlation of structural equation	0.10	

Table 5.4 - Telecommuting Offering Decision (cont.)

Variable Description	estimate	t-statistic
Change in Cost		
Structural Model		
Shared desk available for commuting days	-2.46	-4.58
Reduced salary paid to telecommuters	-0.45	-0.82
Phone bills paid by employer	0.69	1.84
Liability costs paid by employer	0.75	2.73
Highly congested area	-0.76	-2.05
Measurement Model		
Employee direct cost	0.90	3.41
Employee turnover cost	0.17	1.48
Overhead cost	1.92	1.47
τ_{11} (employee direct cost)	-1.14	-4.53
τ_{12} (employee direct cost)	0.71	3.48
τ_{21} (employee turnover cost)	-0.37	-2.83
τ_{22} (employee turnover cost)	1.95	7.23
τ_{31} (overhead cost)	-1.80	-1.71
τ_{32} (overhead cost)	1.48	1.66
Squared multiple correlation structural equation	0.34	
Choice Model		
Telecommuting specific constant	1.17	1.251
Change in productivity	1.84	1.67
Change in costs	-0.50	-1.28
Employees demonstrated interest	2.21	3.10
No experience with telecommuting in organization	-1.095	-1.26
Some experience with telecommuting in the organization	1.80	2.26
Organization is relocating its office	-1.78	-1.93
Number of observation	100	
Complete log-likelihood at convergence	-1401.1	
Log likelihood of choice model at zero	-69.3	
Log likelihood of choice model at convergence	-36.9	
Adjusted rho-squared	0.57	

Given these assumptions, a model of the employee's preferred arrangement is estimated, using the data collected from the menu experiment. Similarly to the employer's program design, a sample is required of the alternatives in the choice set. A sample of 60 alternatives, including the one selected by the employee, is used.

All variables in the specification are dummies, except for the ones related to the minimum and maximum telecommuting frequency, which vary from zero or one to five, respectively. Initially, only the variables in the arrangement attributes are included in the specification. All the estimated coefficients are highly significant, and the signs are all as expected, except for the coefficient related to a higher salary paid to telecommuters, which has a negative sign. This led to the hypothesis that either employees did not have a utility maximization behavior, or that most of the respondents were only considering a constrained choice set, in which a higher salary is not offered, probably reflecting their perception of the most likely employer behavior. Therefore, these alternatives are all excluded from the employee's choice set and the employee's ideal arrangement model does not include a higher salary variable. Behavioral differences due to differences in socio-economics and job characteristics are shown not significant.

The final estimation results, presented in Table 5.5, indicate that employees would strongly prefer to have a flexible telecommuting schedule, with no minimum frequency required and a high maximum frequency allowed. Their preference decreases significantly if a lower salary is offered, or if telework center telecommuting is required. Availability of a computer and access to a computer network significantly increase the preference for an arrangement. Availability of a fax machine and a dedicated phone line increase the preference as well, but not as significantly. Employees prefer arrangements in which the employer pays the phone bills, provides equipment and is liable for property and employee safety.

♦ *PROGRAM CHOICE MODEL*

Given these preferences, the employee needs to select, from the set made available by the employer, the arrangement that best fits her/his preferences. A model is estimated for the employee's choice from this restricted choice set. The explanatory variables in this model are the fitted preference for the offered arrangement and a dummy variable indicating whether a higher salary is offered. The results, presented in Table 5.6, indicate that the probability of an employee selecting an arrangement from the choice set offered by the employer increases as her/his preference for that arrangement increases, and if a higher salary is offered.

Table 5.5 - Employee's Preferred Telecommuting Program

Variable Description	estimate	t-statistic
Minimum telecommuting days per week	-0.69	-57.9
Maximum telecommuting days per week	0.13	13.1
Flexible telecommuting schedule	2.10	60.5
Shared office to work on commuting days	-0.41	-15.5
Shared desk to work on commuting days	-2.54	-48.5
Lower salary to telecommuters	-3.49	-37.5
Telework center-based telecommuting	-2.11	-64.4
Computer available	3.72	64.3
Fax machine available	0.47	18.9
Dedicated phone line available	1.07	38.8
Access to computer network available	2.23	61.1
Required equipment provided by the employer	1.95	58.9
Work-related phone bills paid by the employer	2.25	60.2
Employer is liable for property and employee's health	0.68	26.5
Number of observations	123	
Number of cases	7257	
Log-likelihood at zero	-503.6	
Log-likelihood at convergence	-129.1	
Adjusted rho-squared	0.71	

• *PROGRAM ADOPTION DECISION*

Once the employee selects her/his preferred arrangement from the set available, she/he assesses its impact on lifestyle, work-related costs and income, and decides whether to adopt telecommuting. Initially, separate models of the impact of telecommuting on lifestyle quality and work-related costs are developed. Then, a joint estimation of the latent variable and the choice models is performed. These stages are discussed next.

Table 5.6 - Employee's Telecommuting Program Choice

Variable Description	estimate	t-statistic
Higher salary to telecommuters	0.32	2.08
Fitted value of employee's preference	0.22	14.01
Number of observations	491	
Number of cases	491	
Log-likelihood at zero	-340.3	
Log-likelihood at convergence	-298.8	
Adjusted rho-squared	0.12	

- *Telecommuting Impact on Lifestyle Quality*

♦ *HYPOTHESES*

Telecommuting is expected to influence lifestyle quality by providing the employee with flexibility to adjust her/his schedule to the work load and personal needs and to avoid the commuting burden. The perceived impact is expected to vary according to the characteristics of the individual.

The presence of children in the household is expected to influence differently the perceived impact of the various attributes of the telecommuting arrangement on lifestyle quality. In particular, it is expected that the significance of the flexibility-related variables — minimum and maximum frequencies and telework center indicator — will increase dramatically due to the presence of children in the household. It is also assumed that the job structure will influence the perceived impact of the maximum permitted telecommuting frequency on lifestyle quality.

As far as the measurement model is concerned, it is assumed that different situational constraints have a different impact on the latent variable indicators. Specifically, it is assumed that as household size increases, the expected impact of telecommuting on social life would be less negative. On the other hand, employees working in an individual structure would perceive a negative impact of telecommuting on their social life. The presence of young children in the household would enhance the perceived impact of telecommuting on family life, schedule flexibility, sense of well being and quality of life overall. A job with a team-based structure would negatively affect the perceived impact of telecommuting on group productivity, but positively affect the perceived impact of telecommuting on job autonomy and individual productivity. Finally, individuals in a professional occupation are expected to perceive a less significant impact of telecommuting on schedule flexibility than individuals in other occupations, since they are expected to already have a more flexible arrangement.

♦   *ESTIMATION RESULTS*

The estimation results indicate that establishing a minimum frequency has a negative impact on lifestyle quality, while the more telecommuting days allowed the more beneficial the impact on lifestyle. Telework center telecommuting has a negative impact on lifestyle. The longer the one-way commuting time the more beneficial the impact of telecommuting on lifestyle, mainly for women.

The presence of a child of pre-school age in the household increases the beneficial impact of telecommuting. However, while the presence of young children in the household enhances the significance of the telecommuting arrangement variables, the difference in the same variables for employees with no children in the household is not significant.

The job structure does influence the perceived impact of the maximum allowed telecommuting frequency on lifestyle. While employees working under a team structure perceive lifestyle quality improvements as the maximum frequency increases, employees working primarily on individual tasks perceive a negative impact of high frequencies on lifestyle. This result may represent a need for more schedule flexibility and less interruptions from employees working on a team structure, and a concern about social and professional isolation from employees working individually, even though the maximum number of telecommuting days is not a requirement. Of all the variables included in the measurement models, only the team structure has a significant negative impact on group productivity. The final specification is presented in Table 5.7.

Table 5.7 - Telecommuting Impact on Lifestyle Quality

Variable Description	estimate	t-statistic
Structural Model		
Minimum telecommuting	-0.13	-4.36
Maximum telecommuting, team structure	0.18	2.44
Maximum telecommuting, individual structure	-0.07	-2.94
Telework center telecommuting	-1.19	-13.33
Travel time, female	0.83	5.82
Travel time, male	0.20	1.27
Child under 6 years old in the household	0.75	5.72
Measurement Model		
Social life	0.59	12.99
Family life	0.78	21.82
Job promotion	0.31	6.60
Job security	0.38	8.41
Schedule flexibility	0.75	17.45
Job autonomy	0.58	14.32
Productivity	0.87	24.12
Group productivity	0.62	14.49
- Team structure	-2.01	-2.96
Sense of well being	1.04	32.86
Job satisfaction	1.08	34.38
Life overall	1.00	------
Standard Deviations		
θ_1 (social life)	1.46	30.57
θ_2 (family life)	1.08	29.03
θ_3 (job promotion)	1.54	31.10
θ_4 (job security)	1.48	30.94
θ_5 (schedule flexibility)	1.34	30.06
θ_6 (job autonomy)	1.31	30.59
θ_7 (productivity)	1.03	28.65
θ_8 (group productivity)	1.33	29.94
θ_9 (sense of well being)	0.71	23.94
θ_{10} (job satisfaction)	0.69	22.72
θ_{11} (life overall)	0.74	23.72
Ψ (lifestyle quality latent variable)	1.29	30.13

Table 5.7 - Telecommuting Impact on Lifestyle Quality

Number of observations	491
Squared multiple correlation of structural model	0.27
Log-likelihood at zero	-12556.2
Log-likelihood at convergence	-8912.3

- *Telecommuting Impacts on Work Related Cost*

Changes in an employee's work-related costs under a home-based tele-commuting program include changes in expenses relating to home office utilities, day care costs, transportation, equipment, communications and liability costs. For telework center-based programs, only changes in transportation costs are involved.

♦ *HYPOTHESES*

It is assumed that the expenses of home utilities would increase proportionately to the number of telecommuting days, if the premises would not be used during the day time unless the employee were telecommuting. Day care costs are presumed to increase proportionately to the number of commuting days if the employee has a child of pre-school age and nobody else in the household to look after the child. Commuting costs are expected to increase proportionately to the commuting frequency and to the commuting distance. Overall work-related costs are expected to increase if the employee is required to provide the equipment, pay for phone bills and be liable for property and safety under home-based arrangements.

♦ *SPECIFICATION ISSUES*

Three variables are constructed to assess the change in day care, utilities and transportation costs due to the adoption of telecommuting. The *change in day care cost* variable is created multiplying the current number of commuting days minus the mid-point between the minimum required and the maximum allowed telecommuting by an indicator of whether the employee has no spouse, or the employee's spouse has a paid job, and by an indicator of whether the employee has a child of pre-school age.

The *change in utilities cost* variable is created by multiplying the current number of commuting days minus the mid-point between the minimum required and the maximum allowed telecommuting by an indicator of whether the employee has no spouse, or the employee spouse has a paid job, and by an indicator of whether the employee has no young child.

Two *change in commuting cost* variables are created, one for home-based and one for telework center-based telecommuting programs. These variables multiply the average daily commuting cost by the current number of commuting days minus the mid-point between the minimum required and the maximum allowed telecommuting. Dummy variables are included to indicate the requirement for the employee to provide equipment, pay phone bills and incur liability expenses.

♦ *ESTIMATION RESULTS*

This specification is estimated, and it is verified that there are no statistically significant differences between home- and telework center-based transportation costs. Moreover, it is verified that the only significant telecommuting-related cost refers to the provision of equipment. It is shown that utilities costs increase with telecommuting frequency, but day care costs decrease. Given these results, the final specification is presented in Table 5.8. The measurement model indicates that while day care costs and overall working costs increase, home office utilities costs decrease with commuting frequency, as expected.

• *Telecommuting Adoption Decision*

The model of the employee's choice to adopt telecommuting was estimated jointly with the two latent variable models described above, and two dummy variables, indicating whether a lower or a higher salary was paid to telecommuters. The results of the joint estimation are presented in Table 5.9.

The latent variable models are similar to the ones presented previously, and will not be further discussed. The choice model indicates that telecommuting is preferred to the currently available alternative, other things being equal. If an improvement in lifestyle is expected, the probability of adoption increases. If an increase in work-related costs is expected, the probability of adoption decreases. The negative impact of a lower salary on the employee's choice is much higher than the positive impact of a salary increase.

Table 5.8 - Telecommuting Impact on Work Related Costs

Variable Description	estimate	t-statistic
Structural Model		
Day care costs proxy	0.20	1.48
Home office utilities proxy	-0.26	-2.96
Equipment costs	0.49	2.43
Weekly transportation costs	0.37	2.85
Measurement Model		
Day care costs	0.66	3.20
Home office utilities costs	-0.17	-2.83
Overall working costs	0.68	4.36
Thresholds		
τ_{11} (day care costs)	-1.38	-5.86
τ_{12} (day care costs)	2.93	8.12
τ_{21} (home office utilities costs)	-2.20	-14.14
τ_{22} (home office utilities costs)	0.07	1.17
τ_{31} (overall working costs)	-0.16	-1.77
τ_{32} (overall working costs)	2.00	8.96
Number of observations	440	
Squared multiple correlation of structural equation	0.22	
Log-likelihood at zero	-46929.43	
Log-likelihood at convergence	-1062.20	

Table 5.9 - Employee's Telecommuting Adoption

Variable Description	estimate	t-statistic
Impact on Lifestyle Quality Model		
Structural Model		
Minimum telecommuting	-0.15	-6.56
Maximum telecommuting, team structure	0.10	3.02
Maximum telecommuting, individual structure	-0.04	-1.99
Telework center telecommuting	-1.02	-14.75
Travel time, female	0.69	7.47
Travel time, male	0.27	3.21
Child under 6 years old in the household	0.55	7.46
Measurement Model		
Social life	0.59	11.61
Family life	0.80	18.37
Job promotion	0.32	6.19
Job security	0.41	8.15
Schedule flexibility	0.76	14.40
Job autonomy	0.60	12.51
Productivity	0.92	20.87
Group productivity	0.61	12.43
Sense of well being	1.04	24.86
Job satisfaction	1.07	24.84
Life overall	1.00	------
Standard Deviations		
θ_1	1.43	29.05
θ_2	1.20	28.17
θ_3	1.52	29.48
θ_4	1.45	29.37
θ_5	1.41	28.72
θ_6	1.32	29.12
θ_7	1.02	26.20
θ_8	1.35	29.06
θ_9	0.85	28.81
θ_{10}	0.89	28.07
θ_{11}	0.88	26.24
Ψ	0.85	30.88
Squared multiple correlation of structural model	0.28	

Table 5.9 - Employee's Telecommuting Adoption (cont.)

Variable Description	estimate	t-statistic
Impact on Work Related Cost Model		
Structural Model		
Day care proxy	0.39	2.00
Home office utilities proxy	-0.36	-2.70
Equipment costs	0.76	2.50
Weekly transportation costs	0.65	2.91
Measurement Model		
Day care costs	0.37	4.78
Home office utilities	-0.11	-3.07
Overall working costs	0.50	3.63
Thresholds		
τ_{11} (day care costs)	-1.31	-8.92
τ_{12} (day care costs)	2.88	10.42
τ_{21} (home office utilities costs)	-2.20	-14.15
τ_{22} (home office utilities costs)	0.07	1.17
τ_{31} (overall working costs)	-0.16	-1.67
τ_{32} (overall working costs)	2.19	6.63
Squared multiple correlation for structural equation	0.21	
Choice Model		
Telecommuting specific constant	2.02	8.94
Change in lifestyle quality	0.99	7.01
Change in work-related costs	-0.37	-3.12
Higher salary to telecommuters	0.50	1.12
Lower salary to telecommuters	-2.36	-5.78
Number of observations	440	
Complete log-likelihood at convergence	-9392.83	
Log-likelihood of choice model at zero	-304.99	
Log-likelihood of choice model at convergence	-204.70	
Adjusted rho-squared	0.35	

SUMMARY

In this chapter, a comprehensive behavioral model system is estimated to explain the telecommuting adoption process. Methodologically, this model system uses state-of-the-art demand modeling techniques, allowing for an improved assessment of complex relationships among the relevant variables in both the employer's and the employee's decision processes. Regarding the understanding of the adoption process, this model system:

- incorporates both the employer's and the employee's behavior, providing a more realistic and comprehensive approach to the problem than that taken in previous research.

- demonstrates that the characteristics of the offered telecommuting program vary according to the organization's size and structure. While small organizations adopting a team-based structure prefer arrangements with flexible schedules, large organizations working under an individual task structure prefer arrangements in which the schedule is constrained.

- demonstrates the impact of different telecommuting arrangements on productivity and on the organization's costs, allowing for the configuration of a telecommuting program to address specific motivations. The results indicate that more productivity can be attained if a flexible schedule is allowed. Productivity losses are expected if the employee is paid a lower salary, or if the program is telework center-based. Cost impact is only significant if the arrangement is such that it allows for office space reduction.

- demonstrates the relative impact of changes in profit, motivations and situational constraints on the employer's decision, allowing for a realistic assessment of the effect of various structural changes and policies fostering telecommuting on the level of telecommuting program availability. In particular, the impact of the employees' demand and the employer's exposure to telecommuting are demonstrated to be significant factors on the decision to offer a program.

- demonstrates the impact of different telecommuting arrangements on the employee's lifestyle and work-related costs, as a function of the employee's characteristics and situational constraints, allowing for the configuration of telecommuting programs that address not only transportation-related issues, but also other issues of general concern, such as the integrity of the nuclear family, employment of individuals with socio-economic constraints to mobility, and labor scarcity. The results indicate that females and employees with young children perceive a higher beneficial impact from telecommuting on lifestyle quality than their counterparts. A telework center-based program decreases the beneficial impact.

- demonstrates the significant impact on lifestyle quality, working costs and income changes on the employee's decision to adopt telecommuting.

In the next chapter, a detailed analysis of the results provides a clearer picture of the model applicability.

VI

Analysis of the Results

A discussion of the modeling results and their implications for the design of public and private policies is presented in this chapter. First, the population of interest is identified and the forecasting methodology is explained. Then, the impact of various program designs on the organization and on the household are considered. The current demand for telecommuting is assessed, and the sensitivity of this demand to structural changes and policy is evaluated. Finally, an assessment is provided of the implication of these results for the design of public and private policies.

FORECASTING METHODOLOGY

Assessing the demand for telecommuting involves identifying the population of interest, forecasting the demand for telecommuting under a base case scenario, hypothesizing about potential changes in the base case, and reassessing the demand, given these changes. Each of these stages is discussed in order.

Identifying the Population of Interest

Telecommuting, as defined in this study, is a working arrangement designed for individuals whose primary economic activity involves the creation, processing, manipulation or distribution of information. The vast majority of this labor force is employed in finance, insurance, real estate, services, transportation and public utilities, wholesale and retail trade, and public administration. These employees occupy primarily managerial, professional and administrative support positions, including telemarketing.

According to the U.S.D.O.L. [14], 92.4% of the civilian labor force in the US constitute wage and salaried workers, as opposed to self-employed individuals and unpaid employees. The above mentioned industries employ 76.2% of those wage and salaried workers. Out of this total, 47.9% occupy managerial, professional and administrative support positions. Given these numbers, it is assumed that the fraction of the population for whom telecommuting is feasible at least part-time represent 34% (0.924x0.762x0.479) of the civilian labor force. Out of this total, 54.8% are males, 41.2% are females with no child of pre-school age, and 4% are females with children of pre-school age. About 65% work in small organizations, and 35% work in large organizations employing 50 or more individuals. This population is taken as the basis for extrapolation of the model estimation results.

It should be noted that the model estimation is based on data collected from a convenience sample. As such, the results are subject to bias due to the non-random selection of respondents. The characteristics of the survey distribution process and the limitations of the available data do not allow for the assessment of the full extent of this bias. Ideally, a representative sample with revealed preference data should be collected to verify the accuracy of the predictions. However, an effort is made to diminish the value of the potential bias. In particular, the predictions are weighted to reflect the population shares of small and large organizations, as well as the proportion of male and female employees, with and without young children.

Assessing the Aggregate Demand

Having defined the population of interest, the next step is to predict the share of this population choosing to adopt telecommuting. In order to estimate this share, the sample enumeration method is used, as described below (see Ben-Akiva and Lerman [2] for further details). The probability of a particular arrangement A_i being adopted by an employee is given by:

$$P(A_i|Z_n,O_n) = P_n(A_i \text{ adopted}| \text{offered}, Z_n) *$$
$$P_n(A_i \text{ offered}| \text{designed}, O_n) * P_n(A_i \text{ designed}|O_n) \quad (6.1)$$

where:

$P(A_i|Z_n,O_n)$	= probability of program A_i being adopted by employee n.
$P_n(A_i \text{ adopted}| \text{offered}, Z_n)$	= conditional probability of program A_i being adopted by employee n, given that it was offered by the employer.
$P_n(A_i \text{ offered}| \text{designed}, O_n)$	= conditional probability of a program being offered by the employer of employee n, given that it was designed.
$P_n(A_i \text{ designed}|O_n)$	= probability of a program being designed by the employer of employee n.
Z_n	= characteristics of employee n.
O_n	= characteristics of the employer of employee n.

The program design model is used to calculate the probability of each possible telecommuting arrangement being designed by each employer in the sample. The offering decision model is used to calculate the probability of each designed telecommuting arrangement being offered to the employee.

It is assumed that only one arrangement — if any — is offered to the employee. The telecommuting adoption model then is used to calculate the probability of each telecommuting program being adopted by each employee in the sample, given that it was offered. Given these results, the probability of an employee adopting telecommuting, $P(\text{adoption}|Z_n,O_n)$, is given by:

$$P(adoption|Z_n, O_n) = \sum_{A_i \in A} P(A_i|Z_n, O_n)$$ (6.2)

where A is the set of all possible telecommuting arrangements.

These probabilities are aggregated over each group within the general population, and weighted to estimate the share of the population adopting telecommuting, as follows:

$$W(a) = \sum_{g=1}^{G} \frac{N_g}{N_T} \frac{1}{N_{sg}} \sum_{n=1}^{N_{sg}} P(adoption|Z_n, O_n)$$ (6.3)

where:

$W(a)$ = share of the population choosing to adopt telecommuting.

N_{sg} = number of individuals of group g in the sample.

N_g = number of individuals of group g in the population.

N_T = number of individuals in the population.

The expected value of a specific attribute x_k that constitutes a telecommuting arrangement is given by:

$$E(x_k) = \sum_{g} \frac{N_g}{N_T} \frac{1}{N_{sg}} \sum_{n=1}^{N_{sg}} \sum_{A_i \in A} x_k(A_i) \frac{P(A_i|Z_n, O_n)}{P(adoption|Z_n, O_n)}$$ (6.4)

The sensitivity analysis is performed by changing some values in Z_n and/or O_n, and applying the aggregation method to the new values.

ASSESSING THE DEMAND FOR TELECOMMUTING

In this section, the impact of telecommuting on the organization and on the household is evaluated based on the above methodology. The demand for telecommuting under different scenarios is assessed.

The Employer's Telecommuting Offering Decision

In the first part of this section, the impact of various arrangements on productivity is assessed. Next, the probability of an employer offering a telecommuting program under the current circumstances is calculated, and the sensitivity of this probability to structural changes and policies is evaluated.

- *TELECOMMUTING IMPACT ON PRODUCTIVITY*

Figure 6.1 depicts the impact of different telecommuting programs on productivity. The numbers in Figure 6.1 are obtained by directly applying the results of the *change in productivity* model, presented in Table 5.4, to the scenarios described below.

In Figure 6.1.a, no minimum telecommuting frequency is required, and the maximum telecommuting frequency allowed varies from one to five days per week. The salary paid to telecommuters can be the same or lower than the one they are paid as regular employees, and telecommuting can be home- or telework center-based. In Figure 6.1.b, five telecommuting days per week are allowed, and the minimum frequency required varies from zero to five days per week. (If five telecommuting days are required, it means that the employee will never work in the office. This is already the case, for example, in some telemarketing occupations.) The telecommuters' salary and the telecommuting place vary in a similar manner to that described for Figure 6.1.a. Impact on productivity is measured in a scale from -4, "extremely negative" to +4, "extremely positive."

From Figure 6.1.a, it can be observed that the beneficial impact of telecommuting on productivity increases as the maximum frequency allowed increases. The most favorable impact occurs for home-based arrangements in which the employee is paid the same salary she/he would receive otherwise, no minimum frequency is required and a maximum of five telecommuting days per week is allowed. As explained in Chapter 5, this arrangement provides the maximum flexibility for the employee to adjust her/his schedule to both the work load and personal needs.

Figure 6.1 - Impacts of Telecommuting on Productivity...

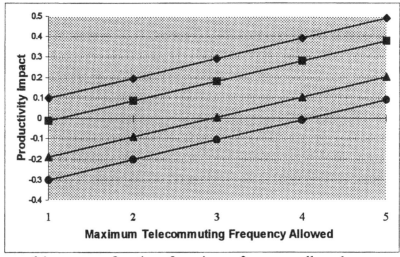

6.1.a - ... as a function of maximum frequency allowed

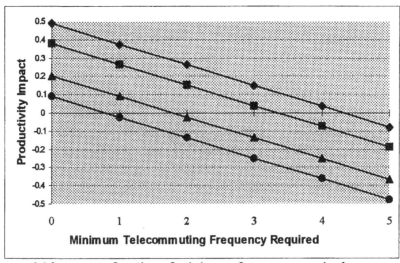

6.1.b - ... as a function of minimum frequency required

Productivity Impact: -4, "extremely negative," to +4, "extremely positive"

Home-based telecommuting is perceived to have a better overall impact on productivity than telework center-based telecommuting. If a lower salary is paid to telecommuters, the negative impact on productivity can only be offset if at least three home-based telecommuting days per week are allowed. If, in addition to involving a lower salary, the telecommuting program is telework center-based, the negative impact on productivity can only be offset if four telecommuting days per week are allowed.

Figure 6.1.b shows that as the minimum telecommuting frequency required increases, the beneficial impact of telecommuting on productivity decreases, and a productivity loss is actually expected, if the employee is constrained to telecommute every day. The negative impact of telecommuting on productivity is aggravated if the program requires telework center telecommuting, and reaches its extreme if, in addition to all these constraints, the employee is paid a lower salary to telecommute.

- *THE OFFERING DECISION*

In this section, the likelihood is calculated of an employer offering a telecommuting program under the current circumstances, based on the methodology described in section 6.1. Then, a sensitivity analysis is conducted to assess how the employer's willingness to offer a telecommuting program varies with structural changes and policies. This analysis is performed using only the models related to the employer's decision process.

The results for the base case scenario, summarized in Table 6.1, indicate that, under current circumstances, 78.7% of the employers in the population of interest would be willing to offer a telecommuting program, representing availability of telecommuting to 26.8% of the labor force. This number and the results that follow represent the weighted probability, to account for the shares of small and large organizations in the population. Even though the survey was distributed to some large organizations located in congested areas, no response was obtained from these organizations. There are no observations in the survey about such organizations. Thus, the predicted potential for adoption of telecommuting may be understated, given that these organizations are very likely to be willing to make telecommuting programs available.

Table 6.1 - Employer's Willingness to Offer Telecommuting

Base Case Scenario	Values
Employers willing to offer telecommuting (sample)	78.7%
Minimum telecommuting frequency required	0.9 days
Maximum telecommuting frequency allowed	2.6 days
Employers offering telework center alternative	26.7%

On average, a minimum of 0.9 telecommuting days per week would be required and a maximum of 2.6 telecommuting days per week would be allowed. However, large organizations adopting an individual task structure would tend to be more restrictive as far as the telecommuting schedule is concerned, requiring a minimum frequency of 2.3 days per week. About 27% of the employers would be willing to offer telework centers as an alternative.

Given this base case, some changes are hypothesized and their impact on the employer's willingness to make a program available are assessed. The synthesis of this analysis is presented in Table 6.2. In this table, the percentage of employers willing to make a telecommuting program available is related to the potential telecommuter population and to the overall labor force. The latter is obtained by multiplying the percentage in the potential telecommuters population by 34%, the share of the total labor force this population represents. The following discussion refers to the telecommuters population, but the same reasoning can be extended to the overall labor force.

In the first scenario, it is hypothesized that the level of congestion in all cities in the sample will increase, reaching the level of the currently highly congested areas, and that organizations will not change location. Under this scenario, the probability that an employer would offer a telecommuting program raises 4.2%, to 82.1%.

However, most of the industries in the surveyed population are location independent, and therefore can relocate entire organizational units to less congested areas relatively easily, if the costs of a central urban location become too steep. Actually, a suburbanization trend has been observed among these service-oriented industries, in the search for both lower location costs and specific labor characteristics (Castells [7]). An obvious step to follow this analysis then is assessing the impact of organization relocation on the decision to make a telecommuting program available.

Table 6.2 - Employer's Willingness to Offer Telecommuting: Sensitivity Analysis

Scenario	Offering		Change
	% of Potential Telecommuters	% of Total Labor Force	(% from base case)
Base case	78.8	26.8	-----
Increase congestion	82.1	27.9	4.3
Increase relocation	59.9	20.4	-23.9
Increase relocation, reduce congestion	59.3	20.2	-24.7
Increase demand	91.3	31.0	16.0
Reduce demand	66.3	22.5	-15.8
Increase information	94.1	32.0	19.6
Increase demand, increase information	98.2	33.4	24.8
All firms under team structure	79.4	27.0	0.9
All firms under individual structure	78.6	26.7	-0.1
All large firms	76.6	26.0	-2.7
All small firms	78.9	26.8	0.3

In the employer's offering decision model there is a dummy variable, indicating whether the organization is currently undergoing a relocation process. To simulate the organization's relocation, this variable is set to one in the forecasting process. First, it is assumed that relocation would not affect the level of congestion of a certain area. If this were the case, the employer's likelihood of offering a telecommuting program would decrease by 23.9%, to 59.9%. If it is assumed that organizations tend to relocate to less congested areas, the added impact of congestion reduction reduces the likelihood of a telecommuting program being offered to 59.3%.

As explained in Chapter 1, one of the primary motivations for an employer to offer a telecommuting program is the increasing need to rely on employees with socio-economic and physical constraints on mobility. If such a situation becomes more pervasive, it is likely that more and more employers will need to deal with employees' demand for more flexible arrangements. In the employer's model, a dummy variable was included if the employees in the organization had demonstrated any interest in telecommuting. In order to simulate an increase in the employees' demand, this variable is set to one for all the respondents in the sensitivity analysis. The new results show that if such an increase in the demand took place, the likelihood of an employer offering a telecommuting program would significantly increase, to 91.3%.

It may be the case, though, that policies will be implemented to release employees' socio-economic constraints to mobility. Such policies would include, for example, more accessible child and elder care services. Assuming that the implementation of such policies reduces the employees' demand for more flexible schedules, the likelihood of an employer offering a telecommuting program would decrease to 66.3%. This result is obtained by setting the dummy variable related to the employees' demand equal to zero in all observations.

As mentioned before, one of the major barriers to a more widespread adoption of telecommuting is managerial concern. Since telecommuting is a novelty, the fear of losing control and incurring severe productivity loses prevents many employers from considering this option. In an effort to eliminate this barrier, the public sector has been investing in demonstration projects, through which employers can gain personal experience with telecommuting, at a relatively low cost, through a short-term commitment.

The impact of such experience on the level of adoption of tele-commuting is captured by two dummy variables included in the em-ployer's model, one indicating that the organization has no previous experience with telecommuting, and one indicating that the organiza-tion has some experience with telecommuting. In order to simulate the impact of the demonstration projects on adoption, the former variable is set to zero and the latter to one in all observations. The results indi-cate that if this type of personal experience is made available to the employer, the likelihood of a program being offered increases signifi-cantly, to 94.1%.

If both information and demand are present, the likelihood of a program being offered rises to 98.2%. Even though this percentage is extremely high, the probability that the required circumstances will be in place for it to be achieved are relatively low. It would imply that employees in all organizations demonstrate interest in telecommuting and that all the organizations have a high level of familiarity with the telecommuting concept.

In addition to these changes in the characteristics of the labor market, the globalization of the economy is inducing organizations to make structural changes in an effort to remain competitive. A shift towards smaller and more flexible organizations has been observed. Under such structures, teams which are formed on an *ad-hoc* basis are the basic functional unit. For employers in such organizations the ability to access the employee when necessary is more important than the employee's physical presence in the office during regular business hours. As such, telecommuting appears to be a very appropriate ar-rangement for these organizations.

Variables indicating whether the employees in the organization work primarily in teams or on individual tasks are included in both the employer's and the employee's models. In order to simulate a shift towards a team structure, all the team-related variables are set to one, and all the individual task-related variables are set to zero in all obser-vations. A shift towards an individual task structure is simulated by setting the individual task variables to their values and the team vari-ables to zero. The sensitivity analysis indicates that a shift towards a team-based structure increases the probability of telecommuting being offered by 0.9%, while a shift towards an individual task structure re-duces this probability by 0.1%. These very modest changes reinforce the previous finding that a change in the organization's structure will impact not so much the willingness to offer a program, but more the characteristics of the program made available.

Large organizations are expected to have a more rigid and bureaucratic structure than small organizations, relying more strongly on the employee's physical presence in the office. A change in the organization's size was simulated by setting the size-related dummy variable in all observations to zero or one, respectively, for all small and all large organizations. As indicated by the result of the sensitivity analysis, a scale growth reduces the likelihood of a program being offered. A scale reduction increases this likelihood, though not significantly, given the high proportion of small organizations in the population.

• *CONCLUSION*

This analysis indicates that telecommuting does have a potential to increase productivity. However, specific arrangements need to be implemented so that this goals can be achieved. In particular, employers perceive that a home-based telecommuting program with a flexible telecommuting schedule and no salary reduction provides the most beneficial impact, while a telework center-based telecommuting program with salary reduction and a constrained schedule has a negative impact on overall productivity.

The potential of telecommuting to reduce costs does not appear significant in this research. The highest potential on this arena lies in the possibility of reducing the use of office space. However, this alternative requires that a large enough number of employees telecommute a large enough number of days per week, so that some of the office space can be vacant all the time. This may require significant constraints to the telecommuting arrangement, to the detriment of the employee's productivity. This result is reflected in the employer's program design model, in which a shared space is preferred less than an individual space for telecommuters to work at on commuting days.

The sensitivity analysis indicates that there is a high willingness to offer a telecommuting program among employers, primarily to address employees' needs. Due to potential bias in the data set, however, these result should be interpreted carefully. A model based on a random sample of organizations may show a less significant willingness to offer telecommuting, and a stronger trend towards the implementation of telecommuting to address cost issues.

It is demonstrated that structural changes and policies may alter the employers' willingness to make a program available. In particular, the flexibility that the service industry has to relocate organizational units to non-congested areas has a significantly negative impact on the employers' decision to offer the program. If no other policy is designed to address employees' socio-economic constraints on mobility, the public sector's support of telecommuting, through the sponsoring of demonstration projects, significantly increases employers' willingness to offer a program providing employees with increased flexibility to address the work load and personal needs. In order to assess how much telecommuting will occur, however, an analysis of the employee's behavior is required.

The Employee's Adoption Decision

The employee's decision to adopt telecommuting is a function of the expected impacts of the available program on lifestyle, work-related costs and income. The discussion about the various aspects of adoption follows.

• *TELECOMMUTING IMPACT ON LIFESTYLE*

Figures 6.2 through 6.4 depict the impact of telecommuting on the employee's lifestyle quality. In each of these figures, the population is divided into four groups, based on gender and on whether the employee is the parent of a child of pre-school age. For each group, the impact of various home- and telework center-based telecommuting arrangements on lifestyle is assessed for individuals working primarily in teams and primarily on individual tasks. The expected impact of telecommuting on lifestyle quality is measured on a scale from -4, "extremely negative" to +4, "extremely positive."

Figure 6.2 - Impact of Telecommuting on Lifestyle Quality
       as a Function of One-Way Commuting Time

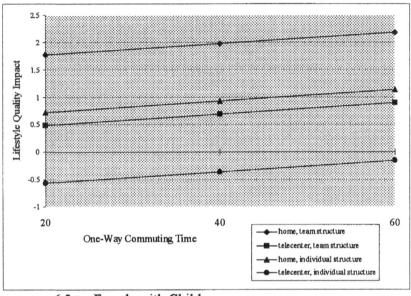

6.2.a - Female with Child

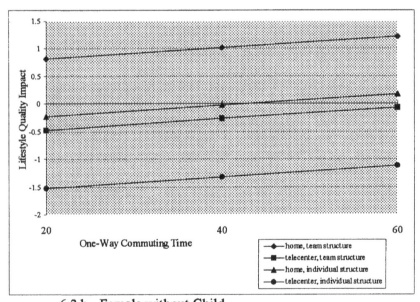

6.2.b - Female without Child

Lifestyle Quality Impact: -4, "extremely negative," to +4, "extremely positive"

Figure 6.2 - Impact of Telecommuting on Lifestyle Quality
as a Function of One-Way Commuting Time (cont.)

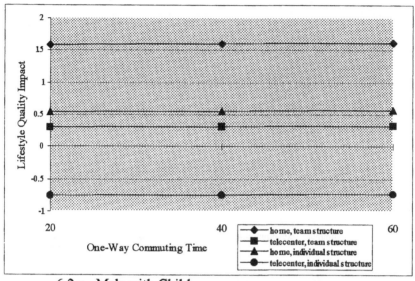

6.2.c - Male with Child

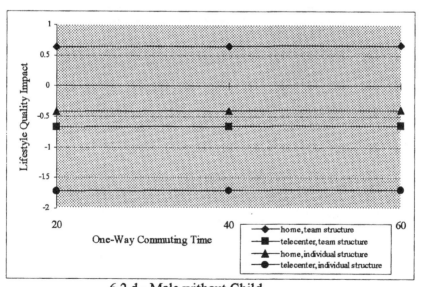

6.2.d - Male without Child

Lifestyle Quality Impact: -4, "extremely negative," to +4, "extremely positive"

Figure 6.3 - Impact of Telecommuting on Lifestyle Quality as a
Function of Minimum Telecommuting Required

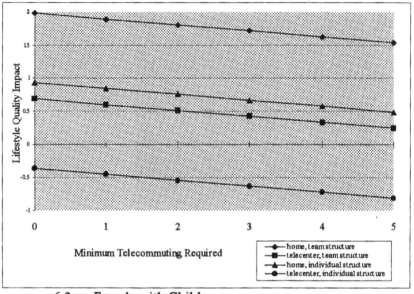

6.3.a - Female with Child

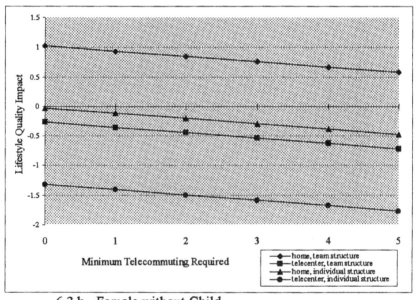

6.3.b - Female without Child

Lifestyle Quality Impact: -4, "extremely negative," to +4, "extremely positive"

Figure 6.3 - Impact of Telecommuting on Lifestyle Quality as a
Function of Minimum Telecommuting Required   (cont.)

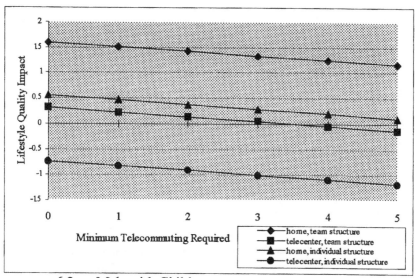

6.3.c - Male with Child

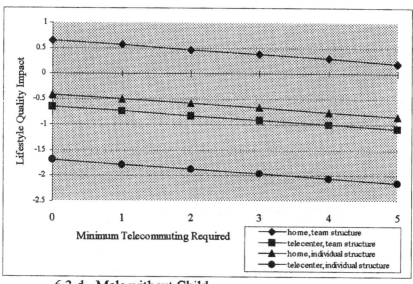

6.3.d - Male without Child

Lifestyle Quality Impact: -4, "extremely negative," to +4, "extremely positive"

Figure 6.4 - Impact of Telecommuting on Lifestyle Quality as a
Function of Maximum Telecommuting Allowed

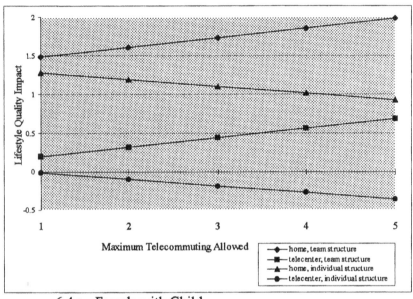

6.4.a - Female with Child

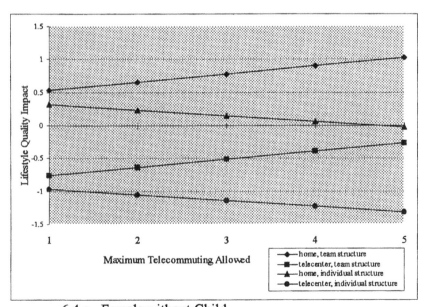

6.4.a - Female without Child

Lifestyle Quality Impact: -4, "extremely negative," to +4, "extremely positive"

Figure 6.4 - Impact of Telecommuting on Lifestyle Quality as a
Function of Maximum Telecommuting Allowed (cont.)

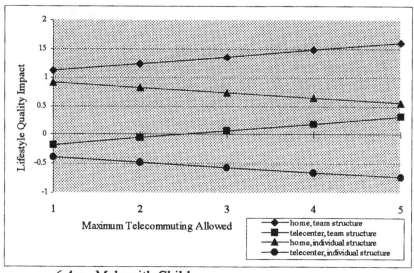

6.4.c - Male with Child

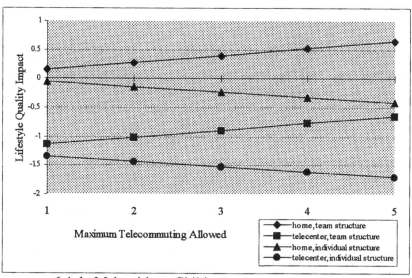

6.4.d - Male without Child

Lifestyle Quality Impact: -4, "extremely negative," to +4, "extremely positive"

In Figure 6.2, the impact of a telecommuting program on lifestyle as a function of the employee's one-way commuting time is shown. For all the arrangements in this figure, no minimum frequency is required, and five telecommuting days per week are allowed. As far as the employee's scheduling is concerned, this non-constrained arrangement offers the maximum flexibility.

This figure indicates that while male employees' perceptions are not sensitive to changes in the one-way commuting time, females perceive an increased beneficial impact from telecommuting on lifestyle as their one-way commuting time increases.

The employee's perception about the impact of a telecommuting arrangement on her/his lifestyle varies significantly according to the characteristics of the individual and of her/his job. If the employee works primarily in a team structure, she/he perceives a positive impact from a home-based, non-constrained, telecommuting program on lifestyle quality. However, if the employee works primarily on individual tasks, the beneficial impact of telecommuting on lifestyle decreases significantly.

At first glance, these results may seem counter-intuitive. However, they may be explained by the fact that employees working primarily in teams are more likely to face many interruptions to their work, and be given less autonomy in their jobs than employees working primarily individually. As such, they are likely to place a higher value on the possibility of working individually, with no interruptions, mainly when a task that requires concentration is to be accomplished. A flexible telecommuting schedule can provide such an alternative, without interfering with the requirements of team work. On the other hand, employees working primarily on individual tasks may need to be present at the work place in order not to feel professionally isolated.

Among those with an individual task structure, a positive impact is perceived only by parents of young children. An exclusively negative impact is perceived by male employees without children.

Telework center-based telecommuting programs are perceived to have some positive impact on lifestyle quality only by parents of young children, working under a team structure. Nevertheless, this benefit is perceived to be significantly inferior to that of a home based program. All other groups expect a negative impact from telecommuting on lifestyle quality with telecommuting from a telework center.

In Figure 6.3, the one-way commuting time is fixed at 40 minutes, five telecommuting days per week are allowed, and the minimum frequency required varies from zero to five. This figure demonstrates the decrease in the beneficial impact of telecommuting on lifestyle as the minimum telecommuting frequency required increases. Requiring any minimum telecommuting frequency has a primarily negative impact on the lifestyle quality of employees with no children and working primarily on an individual task structure. The negative impact is further aggravated if the program is telework center-based. These results may reflect the concern that frequent telecommuting may increase social isolation.

In Figure 6.4, the one-way commuting time is set to 40 minutes, the minimum telecommuting frequency required is set to zero, and the maximum telecommuting frequency allowed varies from one to five. This figure demonstrates that if the employee works primarily on a team-based structure, the positive impact of telecommuting on lifestyle increases as the maximum frequency allowed increases. If the employee works primarily on individual tasks, the positive impact of telecommuting on lifestyle decreases as the maximum frequency allowed increases. This result, as explained previously, indicates that while employees working in a team-based structure may gain autonomy and be less interrupted when telecommuting, employees working on an individual task basis may feel isolated if telecommuting often. However, it is important to realize that even though the survey refers to maximum telecommuting frequency allowed, the results indicate that the respondents may have interpreted it as maximum telecommuting frequency desirable from their own perspective.

Lifestyle quality, as specified in this study, manifests itself through eleven indicators that include various aspects of personal life and career. In Figure 6.5, the sensitivity of each one of these indicators to changes in the latent lifestyle quality is demonstrated.

Figure 6.5.a shows the impact of a home-based program, in which no minimum frequency is required, five telecommuting days per week are allowed, and the salary is the same as that paid to regular commuters, on the lifestyle quality of a female employee with a young child, working in a team structure. Figure 6.5.b shows the impact of a telework center-based program, in which five telecommuting days are required and the salary is lower than that paid to regular commuters, on the lifestyle quality of male employees without children, working

Figure 6.5 - Impact of Telecommuting on Lifestyle Quality Indicators

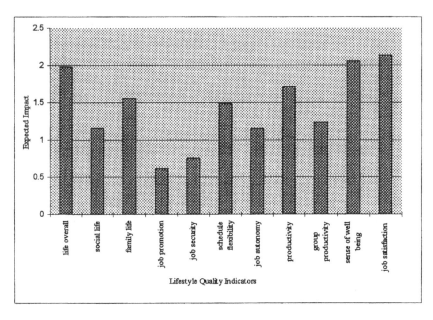

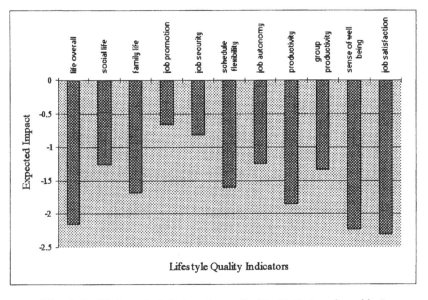

Lifestyle Quality Impact: -4, "extremely negative," to +4, "extremely positive"

primarily on individual tasks. These two groups represent the extremes on the spectrum of the perceived impact of telecommuting on lifestyle. In this figure, the one-way commuting time is set to 40 minutes.

This figure indicates that aspects related to job security and group productivity are less sensitivety to changes in the characteristics of the telecommuting arrangement than aspects related to personal life and individual productivity. However, the direction of this impact varies according to the characteristics of the individual and of her/his job.

- *THE ADOPTION DECISION*

A sensitivity analysis is performed to provide a better understanding of the employee's responses to changes in the levels of various attributes of a telecommuting program. In this analysis, only the employee's adoption model is used, and the telecommuting program designed by the employee is taken as the base case. The results, presented in Table 6.3, relate the percentage of adopters both to the potential telecommuter population and to the overall labor force. This analysis is for the potential telecommuters population, but the same reasoning applies to the labor force as a whole.

The results show that about 83.6% of the employees in the potential telecommuters population who are offered the telecommuting arrangement they designed would be willing to telecommute, representing 28.4% of the civilian labor force. If the employer pays for all telecommuting costs, this percentage increases to 85.9%. This percentage, higher than the base case, may indicate that some of the respondents did not adopt a utility maximizing behavior when designing their ideal telecommuting program or did not include alternatives in which the telecommuting costs were paid by the employer in their choice set.

If the employee needs to pay for all telecommuting costs, the percentage of employees willing to adopt telecommuting decreases to 83.2%. Even though this change may seem very modest, it should be noted that the most significant telecommuting cost involves the acquisition of a computer, which in many cases is already available in the household. If only telework center-based programs are available, the percentage of employees willing to adopt telecommuting decreases 20.1%, to 66.8%. If all programs are home-based, the percentage of adoption increases to 85.9%.

Employees are extremely sensitive to a reduction in their income level. If a lower income is offered in exchange for the permission to telecommute, the percentage of employees willing to adopt telecommuting decreases 55.3%, to 37.4%. A salary increase induces a small 5.3% increase in the percentage of employees willing to adopt telecommuting. If employees are offered a highly flexible program, in which no minimum frequency is required and five telecommuting days per week are allowed, the adoption probability increases to 84.2%. If employees are constrained to telecommute only two days per week, which may be the situation in a program to address traffic problems, the probability of adoption decrease 2.4%, to 81.6%.

If congestion level increases, and the one-way commuting time increases 20 minutes, the willingness to adopt telecommuting increases 2%, indicating the relatively low significance of commuting time on employees' telecommuting preference. If a team structure prevails, the likelihood of an employee adopting telecommuting increases 5.9%, while if an individual task structure prevails, the percentage of employees willing to adopt telecommuting decreases 0.6%.

- *CONCLUSION*

This analysis indicates that employees' perceptions about the impact of telecommuting on lifestyle changes significantly according to the arrangement attributes and to the characteristics of the employee and of her/his job. Overall, a home-based arrangement with an unconstrained schedule results in the most favorable impact on lifestyle, while a telework center-based arrangement with a constrained schedule produces the least favorable results.

Parents of young children have a more positive response to the impact of telecommuting on lifestyle than employees without young children. Similarly, female employees perceive a more positive impact from such an arrangement on lifestyle than their male counterparts.

Table 6.3 - Employee's Conditional Probability of Adoption - Sensitivity Analysis

Scenario	Adoption		Change
	% of potential telecommuters	% of total labor force	(% from base case)
Base case	83.6	28.4	-----
All costs paid by employer	85.9	29.2	2.8
All costs paid by employee	83.2	28.3	0.5
Telework center only	66.8	22.7	20.1
Home only	85.9	29.2	2.8
Lower salary offered	37.4	12.7	-55.3
Same salary offered	82.4	28.0	-1.4
Higher salary offered	88.1	30.0	5.3
Minimum zero, maximum five days	84.2	28.6	0.7
Minimum two, maximum two days	81.6	27.7	-2.4
Travel time +10 minutes	84.5	28.7	1.0
Travel time +20 minutes	85.3	29.0	2.0
Team structure	88.5	30.0	5.9
Individual structure	83.1	28.3	-0.6

Employees working in a team structure perceive a primarily positive impact from telecommuting on lifestyle, while employees working individually perceive a mostly negative impact.

These results are in agreement with the employer's perceptions about the negative impact of constrained flexibility on productivity, and expands this conclusion, pointing to the need to understand the motivations and constraints the employee faces in adopting telecommuting, before a successful program can be designed.

The analysis also demonstrates that employees are extremely sensitive to salary reductions. If a lower salary is paid to telecommuters, the probability of adoption drops drastically.

Assessing the Demand for Telecommuting

In order to be able to assess the actual demand for telecommuting, a joint forecast needs to be performed of the employer's willingness to offer telecommuting and the employee's willingness to adopt a program, given the offer. Table 6.4 shows the base case for this forecast, for the potential telecommuter population as a whole and the population segments, divided according to gender and the presence of a young child in the household.

Table 6.4 - Demand for Telecommuting - Base Case Scenario

Population Segment	Adoption (%)	Min. Freq.	Max. Freq.	Telecenter (%)
Total	45.8	0.6	1.5	11.6
Female with child	61.7	0.8	1.9	16.7
Female without child	53.8	0.7	1.8	12.8
Male with child	43.5	0.6	1.4	12.1
Male without child	38.2	0.4	1.3	10.1

The results indicate that females are more likely than males to adopt telecommuting. Parents of young children are more likely than other employees to adopt telecommuting. On average, 45.8% of the potential telecommuter population would adopt telecommuting under the current circumstances, representing 15.6% of the overall labor force. The expected minimum telecommuting frequency in the population is 0.6 days per week, and the expected maximum telecommuting frequency in the population is 1.5 days per week. About 11.6% of the telecommuting would be telework center-based and the remaining 88.4% would be home-based.

Given that the average employee commutes five days per week, and that the surveyed population represents about 34% of the civilian labor force, and taking the mid-range of the expected telecommuting frequency interval as a basis, these number indicate the potential of telecommuting to eliminate approximately 6.0% (1/5x0.34x0.884) of the total number of weekly commuting trips and to reduce the commuting distance for 0.8% (1/5x0.34x0.116) of total commuters, under the current scenario. The impact of this reduction on the transportation system, however, depends on how these trips are distributed over the week and during the day. For example, if telecommuting is more likely to occur on particular days of the week, while traffic on those days may be reduced, no difference will be noticed in traffic on other days. If the trips that do not happen due to telecommuting would otherwise take place during peak hours, a 6.0% reduction would be significant. If, however, these telecommuters work under a flexi-time schedule, in which they are not required to commute during peak hours, the impact of telecommuting on congestion in the transportation system may actually be insignificant.   A sensitivity analysis is performed to verify how these estimates respond to structural changes and policies. The results are presented in Table 6.5. An increase in the congestion level of currently non-congested areas would lead to a 3.1% increase in the level of adoption of telecommuting. The relocation of organizations to areas of low congestion reduces the demand for telecommuting in 15.5%, to 38.7% of adoption within the telecommuter population. An increase in employees' requests to telecommute increases telecommuting adoption by 10.7%.

An increase in the level of experience employers have with telecommuting raises the adoption level to 79.2%. This result is obtained by setting the dummy variable indicating the organization's experience with telecommuting to one for all observations. Even though this level of experience in the population may seem unlikely, this result certainly points to the importance of the public sector's investment on demonstration projects to increase the level of telecommuting.

Table 6.5 - Demand for Telecommuting - Sensitivity Analysis

Scenario	Adoption		Change
	% of potential telecommuters	% of total labor force	(% of base case)
Base case	45.8	15.6	----
Increase congestion	47.2	16.0	3.1
Increase relocation	38.9	13.2	-15.1
Increase relocation, reduce congestion	47.9	16.3	4.6
Increase demand	50.7	17.2	10.7
Increase information	79.2	26.9	72.9
Reduce information	20.6	7.0	-55.0
Increase demand, increase information	81.6	27.7	78.2
Team structure	50.9	17.3	11.1
Individual structure	45.5	15.5	-0.6
Small firms	46.1	15.7	0.7
Large firms	42.7	14.5	-6.8
Invert proportion male/female in the labor force	47.4	16.1	3.5

An increase in the adoption of team structures increases the demand in 11.1%, to 50.9%, while if a primarily individual task structure is adopted, the demand decreases 6.8%, down to 45.5% of adoption. These results may, initially, seem counterintuitive. However, it should be noted that these proportions refer to the level of adoption, not to the characteristics of the adopted program. Individuals working primarily in teams are likely to face many interruptions to their work in the office, and thus feel they sometimes need privacy to be able to concentrate better and be more productive. A flexible telecommuting arrangement, in which this privacy is granted without interfering with the team work, would be most desirable. On the other hand, individuals who work primarily on individual tasks may need to be present in the office to enhance their sense of belonging to that community.

Considering the current trend in the labor market, a scenario is considered in which the proportion of males and females in the labor force is inverted. The results indicate that, under these circumstances, the demand would increase to 47.4%.

SUMMARY

This chapter estimates the demand for telecommuting and assesses its sensitivity to policies and to changes in the characteristics of the organization's environment, including the labor market, location costs and congestion. The results indicate that the potential volume of telecommuting is large enough to deserve the attention of the public sector. It has been demonstrated that:

- relocation is a substitute for telecommuting, and to the extent that it is a feasible solution for organizations, it will reduce the demand for telecommuting. Specifically, it is expected that the suburbanization of the services industry will negatively affect telecommuting demand.

- addressing employees' needs is one of the primary motivations for employers to adopt telecommuting. Given that the proportion of individuals with socio-economic mobility constraints in the labor force has been increasing, the tendency is for this demand to grow, unless some policy to address employees' mobility constraints is implemented successfully.

- changes in the organization's size and structure do not influence adoption as significantly as they influence the characteristics of the available programs. Large organizations in which the employees work primarily on individual tasks offer arrangements with less schedule flexibility than small organizations, or organizations in which the employees work primarily in teams.

- a telecommuting program can be designed in such a way that it yields increases in productivity. Nevertheless, it is essential that the employee's willingness to telecommute be respected. Employees with family commitments, or employees working in a team structure are more likely to be willing to telecommute than their counterparts. Telecommuters are extremely sensitive to a salary reduction, and such a design may yield significant productivity losses.

- a generalized negative perception about telework centers is present among employers and employees. It is, therefore, important that some research be conducted to identify the market for such arrangements, so that the investments of the public sector to foster their adoption can be effective.

- under the current circumstances, telecommuting has the potential to eliminate 6.0% of work trips, and can reduce the travel time of another 0.8%. The extent to which these changes may impact the transportation system, however, depends on the current and future commuting patterns of potential telecommuters.

- the likelihood of an employer offering a telecommuting program significantly increases as her/his level of exposure to such arrangements increases. This important result validates the public sector support for demonstration projects as an effective policy to increase telecommuting adoption.

VII

Conclusion

In this chapter, an assessment of the contribution of this research to the state of the art is provided and directions for further research are suggested.

CONTRIBUTIONS TO THE STATE OF THE ART

This research contributes to the state of the art in demand modeling applications by modeling the adoption of telecommuting, and by furthering understanding of the telecommuting adoption process. It contributes to demand modeling techniques by:

- developing two applications of simultaneous estimation of discrete choice and latent variable models with continuous, discrete and ordered categorical indicators. These models, of the employer's offering decision and the employee's adoption decision, contain more information, and allow for a clearer behavioral interpretation than simple discrete choice models.

- presenting applications of modeling using menu data in the employer's program design model and in the employee's preferred program model. A menu type of survey permits the respondent to consider a larger choice set than that provided by a fractional factorial experimental design. The modeling process permits the estimation of interactions between attributes of the arrangement, and the use of a large choice set enhances the significance of the model's coefficients.

The research contributes to an understanding of the telecommuting adoption process by:

- developing and demonstrating a comprehensive behavioral model, incorporating both the employer's and the employee's perspectives. The employer is assumed to have a profit maximization behavior; the employee is assumed to have a utility maximizing behavior. Given these assumptions, the design of a telecommuting program is modeled as a function of the motivations and constraints faced by the organization, and the employer's decision to make telecommuting available is modeled as a function of the expected impact of the designed program on productivity and costs. The employee's choice of a telecommuting program is modeled as a function of her/his motivations and constraints, and the decision to adopt telecommuting as a function of the potential impact of the program on the employee's lifestyle, work-related costs and income.

- using an innovative survey instrument, in which both employers and employees are presented with a full profile of telecommuting. With this approach, respondents can experience the actual complexity of the adoption decision process in their choice tasks. To create a more realistic choice context, both employers and employees are given the opportunity to design their preferred telecommuting program, rather than only being presented with alternatives designed by the researcher.

- applying state of the art demand modeling techniques to devise comprehensive measures for the impact of a telecommuting arrangement on (i) productivity, incorporating individual and group productivity, as well as supervisory capabilities, (ii) the organization's costs, including equipment, telecommunication, overhead and employee direct and indirect costs, (iii) the employee's lifestyle quality, including career, family and social life, and (iv) the employee's working costs, including transportation, telecommunications, liabilities, home utilities and child care expenses.

The following insights into the adoption process are gained through this study:

- It is demonstrated that the ideal telecommuting program depends on the characteristics of the organization and on the employer's motivations and constraints to adopt telecommuting. For example, small organizations prefer a program with a flexible schedule, while large organizations prefer a fixed telecommuting schedule. Organizations adopting a team-based structure are unlikely to require a minimum telecommuting frequency, and would restrict the number of telecommuting days allowed per week. Organizations adopting an individual task structure are likely to require a minimum telecommuting frequency, and would be more likely to allow for up to five telecommuting days per week.

- It is demonstrated that the impact of telecommuting on productivity is a function of the flexibility that is provided to the employee to address her/his work load and personal needs. It is also shown that the potential of telecommuting to reduce the organization's costs is limited, unless a large enough number of employees telecommute often enough to free up some office space. An overall negative perception of telework centers among employers is identified.

- It is demonstrated that the impact of telecommuting on lifestyle depends on the characteristics of the employee and of her/his job. For example, parents of young children are more likely to perceive an improvement in lifestyle quality due to telecommuting than individuals with no young children. An individual working primarily in a team perceives more beneficial impacts of telecommuting on lifestyle than an individual working primarily on individual tasks. A negative attitude toward telework centers among employees is identified.

- Various telecommuting policies are tested and guidelines are provided for both the public and the private sectors to foster the adoption process. It is demonstrated that the necessity of addressing the employee's needs is one of the major motivations for the adoption of telecommuting. An increase in the level of information about telecommuting available to employers, in conjunction with the design of programs that actually address the employee's needs, may increase adoption significantly. Differences in the organization's scale and structure do not significantly impact the level of adoption, but they do change the characteristics of the available programs, with large organizations working with an individual task structure preferring rigid telecommuting schedules.

The level of understanding of the telecommuting adoption process has thus been enhanced. Nevertheless, many issues are still to be addressed and should be the focus of further research.

RESEARCH DIRECTIONS

Telecommuting is only one of the many changes affecting organizations and households due to the revolution in information technology and telecommunications. As such, its potential impact on the transportation system should be analyzed within the broader context in which all these changes are taking place. Potential areas of research to address these issues are presented below, in reference to the travel demand model system presented in Figure 1.1.

Urban and Regional Development

At the urban and regional development level, two primary areas of research are foreseen. As far as infrastructure provision is concerned, the availability of fiber optics to the household significantly increases the type of tasks that can be performed remotely, enhancing the potential market for telecommuting. The availability of this infrastructure expands not only the type of job tasks, but also other types of activities that can be performed at home, such as entertainment and shopping. Thus, it is expected to significantly affect the way households use the urban space, and consequently the transportation system. This aspect of the information technology revolution should be the subject of extensive study.

Regarding the organization's decisions, telecommuting is only one of the multiple alternatives available to address issues such as scarcity of labor, high costs of location, or the need to reduce traffic congestion. Alternatives to each one of these issues should be compared with telecommuting. For example, if telecommuting is being considered primarily to reduce locations costs, relocation may be an alternative to be considered. If the objective is to reduce labor costs, a shift to contracted work may be more efficient. If the goal is to address traffic mitigation mandates, a policy to encourage car-pooling may be more in line with the manager's objectives. Therefore, a more detailed analysis of the motivations employers have for considering telecommuting and of the alternatives available may yield very illuminating results into the adoption process.

Moreover, in some situations telecommuting may not be possible, given the current definition of jobs and tasks. It may be the case, though, that jobs and tasks can be redesigned in such a way that the market for telecommuting increases significantly. For example, the results of this study indicate that telecommuting can address the needs of employees working primarily in teams if the telecommuting schedule is flexible enough to be adjusted to the weekly work load. Team meetings can therefore be schedule in such a way that telecommuting will actually be beneficial to each individual, enhancing the overall productivity of the group.

Household Decisions

At the level of the household, telecommuting affects long term and short term decisions. It influences the individual's decision to join the labor market and the characteristics of her/his chosen arrangement. It may change the required housing characteristics and the choice of house location. Given that the employee's primary location under telecommuting may be the home, the characteristics of the set of available activities in which the individual can engage changes. The automobile availability is affected, freeing one vehicle for more trips to be made. As a consequence of this impact on lifestyle and accessibility choices, the household use of the urban space, and in particular of the transportation system, is altered.

The increased flexibility provided to individuals by telecommuting may alter her/his daily decisions about activity sequencing, travel time and travel mode. In particular, telecommuting may significantly enhance the value of the information provided by Advanced Traveler's Information Systems, since the employee is given the freedom to alter her/his trip plans.

Eventually, transportation planners should be interested in the potential impact of telecommuting on the performance of the transportation system. As such, the impact of the availability of telecommuting on all the stages of the travel decision-making process needs to be addressed.

It should be emphasized that telecommuting is only a small part of the overall information technology revolution. The innovations brought about by this revolutionare expected to significantly influence organizations' and households' use of the urban space. As such, it is crucial that the travel demand model system be expanded to incorporate the impact not only of telecommuting but of all other information technology alternatives to activity performance, at all of its levels.

Additional Steps for this Study

This study represents a first step towards an understanding of the overall adoption process. As such, it has some limitations and many improvements should be made on it in further research. In order to enhance forecasting potential, a more well-defined approach is required to various job categories, organizational structures and working arrangements. In particular, a more detailed definition of the meaning of *team work* would significantly improve on the results presented herein. A better characterization of the tasks individuals perform in their jobs would allow for a more refined definition of information workers. Such characterization at the population level would also significantly improve the quality of these results.

Furthermore, the limitations of the data set used in this study should be recognized. Though it provides useful information on the telecommuting adoption process, it is based on a convenience sample, and therefore is limited in its potential for generalization. A similar modeling effort with a more representative data set would significantly enhance the forecasting power of this system.

Finally, the results have indicated that an increase in the level of information significantly increases the level of adoption of telecommuting. A more detailed study, based on data collected before and after the organization's experience with telecommuting, would shed more light on the impact of information about and experience with telecommuting on employers' and employees' attitudes, preferences and behavior.

A - The Employer's Survey

MANAGER'S TELECOMMUTING SURVEY

DEFINING TELECOMMUTING

Telecommuting refers to working arrangements in which the office worker is allowed or required to work at home or at a telework center on a regular basis, during regular working hours, full- or part-time, maintaining contact with the central office through telecommunications devices. A telework center is a facility located near the worker's home, where the necessary office infrastructure is provided by a third party at an agreed rate.

YOUR EXPERIENCE WITH TELECOMMUTING

1. When did you first hear about telecommuting?
   _____ days , _____ months, _____ years ago

2. How often have you received information about it, since then?
   ( ) very often   ( ) often
   ( ) occasionally   ( ) never

3. What kind of experiences have you had with telecommuting (choose as many as apply)?
   ( ) none   ( ) from the organization I work for
   ( ) from readings   ( ) from the group I supervise
   ( ) from an organization I have contact with
   ( ) other: _____

4. Why would (do) you offer a telecommuting program to the employees you supervise?

	definitely not								definitely yes
To increase their productivity	1	2	3	4	5	6	7	8	9
To address their personal needs	1	2	3	4	5	6	7	8	9
To reduce labor costs (turnover, sick leave	1	2	3	4	5	6	7	8	9
To reduce/avoid overhead expenses	1	2	3	4	5	6	7	8	9
To attract skilled employees	1	2	3	4	5	6	7	8	9
Other: _____	1	2	3	4	5	6	7	8	9
I wouldn't offer a telecommuting program	1	2	3	4	5	6	7	8	9

5. Is there a telecommuting program currently available to the employees you supervise?
   ( ) yes   ( ) no

THE GROUP YOU SUPERVISE

6. How many salaried employees do you currently supervise? _____

7. How many independent contractors do you currently supervise?_____

8. In what kind of structure do the salaried employees you supervise work?
    ( ) mostly in teams
    ( ) mostly performing individual tasks, within a team structure
    ( ) mostly on individual projects

DESIGNING A TELECOMMUTING PROGRAM

Consider the possibility of making telecommuting available to the group you supervise. In this section we ask you to design this program. Assume that:

- employees' participation is voluntary
- participating employees will receive the same basic benefits they receive as regular employees
- participating employees will work under the same schedule (full- or part-time) they currently work

Your telecommuting program will be characterized by the following attributes:

Attributes which apply to ANY telecommuting program:

- Minimum: minimum number of days per week telecommuting will be required
- Maximum: maximum number of days per week telecommuting will be allowed
- Schedule: fixed, if the employee is required to telecommute always on the same weekday; flexible if the employee can vary the weekday on which he/she telecommutes
- Work space: work space available to telecommuters when at the main office
- Salary: variation in telecommuter's salary compared to regular employee's
- Place: site from where telecommuting is performed (home or tele-work center)

Attributes which apply to HOME-BASED telecommuting only:

- Equipment: equipment and/or telecommunications services required for telecommuting
- Equipment provider: party who provides the required equipment and services
- Phone bill: party who pays the work-related home phone bills
- Liability: party financially responsible for work-related accidents during telecommuting time

Attributes which apply to TELEWORK CENTER telecommuting only:

If you choose to design a program which is telework center-based, assume that the telework center provides each employee with a computer equipped with basic office software, a laser printer and a telephone. In addition, they have access to a computer network and a fax machine at a daily rate of $150 per telecommuter.

YOUR TELECOMMUTING PROGRAM

If there is a telecommuting program currently available to the employees you supervise, please refer to it when answering the following questions.[1]

9. How many of the employees you supervise occupy a MANAGERIAL POSITION?_____ employees

If none of the employees you supervise occupies a managerial position, go to question 13.

10. What percentage of these employees have demonstrated some interest in telecommuting?_____%

11. What percentage have formally requested to telecommute? _____%

---

[1] A similar set of question was asked related to employees on managerial, professional and administrative support positions.

12. How would you design a telecommuting program for these employees?

Minimum(days/week):	( ) 0 ( ) 1 ( ) 2 ( ) 3 ( ) 4 ( ) 5
Maximum(days/week):	( ) 1 ( ) 2 ( ) 3 ( ) 4 ( ) 5
Schedule:	( ) fixed ( ) flexible
Work space:	( ) individual office ( ) shared office ( ) shared desk
Salary:	( ) __% lower ( ) same ( ) __% higher
Place:	( ) home ( ) telework center ( ) either

The following refer to home-based telecommuting only:

Equipment:	( ) computer ( ) fax ( ) dedicated phone ( ) network access ( ) other: _____
Equipment provider:	( ) employer ( ) employee
Phone bills:	( ) employer ( ) employee
Liability:	( ) employer ( ) employee

a. Would the organization you work for actually offer this telecommuting arrangement to your employees?   ( ) yes   ( ) no

b. How many of these employees do you believe would adopt this arrangement?_____ employees

c. How would you expect the following issues to vary under this arrangement:
Employees' productivity
( ) increase _____% ( ) remain the same ( ) decrease _____%
Direct costs per employee
( ) increase _____% ( ) remain the same ( ) decrease _____%
Employee turnover expenses
( ) increase _____% ( ) remain the same ( ) decrease _____%
Overhead costs
( ) increase _____% ( ) remain the same ( ) decrease _____%

d. What type of impact would you expect this arrangement to have on:

	extremely negative							extremely positive	
These employees' job satisfaction	1	2	3	4	5	6	7	8	9
The team spirit	1	2	3	4	5	6	7	8	9
The quality of telecommuters' work	1	2	3	4	5	6	7	8	9
The quality of the group's work	1	2	3	4	5	6	7	8	9
Your ability to manage these employees	1	2	3	4	5	6	7	8	9
Your ability to evaluate telecommuters' performance	1	2	3	4	5	6	7	8	9
Your ability to attract qualified employees	1	2	3	4	5	6	7	8	9

e. The overall impact of this arrangement on the organization would be:
( ) positive   ( ) neutral   ( ) negative

ABOUT THE ORGANIZATION YOU WORK FOR

13. What industry do you work in?
( ) Banking and Finance   ( ) Telecommunication
( ) Real Estate   ( ) Computer Software/Hardware
( ) Business Services   ( ) Education
( ) Government   ( ) Other: _____
( ) Consultancy

14. Location of your work place(state, city and zip code): _____
15. How long has your office been located at this site? ___ years

16. What type of office is this?
( ) headquarters   ( ) sales   ( ) divisional branch
( ) support services   ( ) other: _____

17. What type of market does your organization address?
( ) local   ( ) national   ( ) regional   ( ) international

18. What was your organization's revenue in the last fiscal year?___dollars
19. How many salaried employee are currently on the payroll of your organization? _____ employees

20. Is your organization currently undergoing any of the following processes?
( ) expanding scale   ( ) re engineering
( ) reducing scale   ( ) relocating

B - The Employee's Survey

EMPLOYEE'S TELECOMMUTING SURVEY

DEFINING TELECOMMUTING

Telecommuting refers to working arrangements in which the office worker is allowed or required to work at home or at a telework center on a regular basis, during regular working hours, full- or part-time, maintaining contact with the central office through telecommunications devices. A telework center is a facility located near the worker's home, where the necessary office infrastructure is provided by a third party.

YOUR TELECOMMUTING PROGRAM

1. Is your job suitable for telecommuting?   ( ) yes   ( ) no (go to 13)

2. Is telecommuting available to you at the company you work for?
   ( ) yes   ( ) no (go to 13)

3. Is the participation in this program voluntary? ( ) yes   ( ) no

4. Where do employees telecommute from?
   ( ) home   ( ) telework center   ( ) either

5. How many days per week is telecommuting allowed?
   minimum _____ days per week
   maximum _____ days per week

6. Are employees required to telecommute on the same schedule every week?   ( ) yes   ( ) no

7. What equipment or services does <u>your employer</u> provide for telecommuters' use?
   ( ) none   ( ) dedicated phone line
   ( ) personal computer ( ) access to computer network
   ( ) fax   ( ) other: _____

8. What equipment or services are <u>telecommuters</u> required to provide themselves?
   ( ) none   ( ) dedicated phone line
   ( ) personal computer ( ) access to computer network
   ( ) fax   ( ) other: _____

9. Who pays for the work-related phone bills?
 ( ) your employer ( ) shared
 ( ) the telecommuters ( ) no work-related phone bills

10. How does a telecommuter's salary compare to that of an employee in
 the same position who does not telecommute?
 ( ) it is the same as that of a regular employee
 ( ) it is _____% higher than that of a regular employee
 ( ) it is _____% lower than that of a regular employee

11. Are you currently a telecommuter? ( ) yes ( ) no (go to 13)

12. How many days did you telecommute during your most recently
 completed work week? _____ days

13. Why would (do) you telecommute?

	definitely not							definitely yes	
To spend more time with your family	1	2	3	4	5	6	7	8	9
To be more productive	1	2	3	4	5	6	7	8	9
To have more flexibility	1	2	3	4	5	6	7	8	9
To have more job autonomy	1	2	3	4	5	6	7	8	9
To reduce your child care expenses	1	2	3	4	5	6	7	8	9
To reduce your elder care expenses	1	2	3	4	5	6	7	8	9
Other: _____	1	2	3	4	5	6	7	8	9
You wouldn't telecommute	1	2	3	4	5	6	7	8	9

YOUR WORKING WEEK

The following questions refer to your most recently completed work week.

14. How many days did you work, in total? _____ days

15. How many of these days did you work
 at home, during business hours? _____ days
 at home, after business hours? _____ days
 in your office? _____ days
 elsewhere? _____ days

If you did not work in your office during this week, go to question 22.

16. What transportation mode did you most frequently use to get to your office?
    ( ) car (drive alone)   ( ) bus
    ( ) carpool   ( ) commuter rail
    ( ) subway   ( ) other: _____

17. How many days did you come directly from home?   _____ days

18. What was your average one-way commuting time?   ____ h, ___ min.
    minimum one-way commuting time?   ____ h, ___ min.
    maximum one-way commuting time?   ____ h, ___ min.

19. How many hours per day did you work at your office?   ____ h

20. What percentage of your time in your work place was spent in:
    face-to-face interactions with customers   _____%
    individual project tasks: _____%
    team project tasks, working individually: _____%
    team project tasks, working in groups: _____%

21. How much did you spend on your commute during this week?
    gasoline: _____
    parking: _____
    transit: _____
    other: _____
    TOTAL: _____ dollars

22. What is the one-way commuting distance between your home and office?   _____ miles

DESIGNING A TELECOMMUTING PROGRAM

Suppose the company you work for were considering implementing a telecommuting program. In this section we present some telecommuting arrangements which could be made available for your consideration. In each scenario, assume that:
- your participation in the telecommuting program is voluntary.
- if participating, you will receive the same benefits you receive as a regular employee.

- if participating, you will work under the same schedule (full- or part-time) you currently work.
- all other aspects of your working arrangement which are not mentioned below remain the same as now.

The attributes of each scenario have the following meanings:

Attributes which apply to ANY scenario:
- Minimum: minimum number of days per week you will be required to telecommute
- Maximum: maximum number of days per week you will be allowed to telecommute
- Schedule: fixed, if you are required to telecommute always on the same weekdays; flexible if you can vary the weekdays on which you telecommute
- Work space: space available for your use in the main office
- Salary: variation in your current salary due to telecommuting
- Place: site from where telecommuting is performed (home or telework center)

Attributes which apply to HOME-BASED telecommuting only:
- Equipment: minimum equipment required for telecommuting
- Equipment provider: party responsible for providing the equipment
- Phone bills: party responsible for paying the work-related phone bills
- Liability: party financially responsible for work-related accidents during telecommuting

Attributes which apply to TELEWORK CENTER telecommuting only:
- Equipment: equipment available in the telework center

All the expenses related to the telework center are paid by the employer. Whenever a computer is available in the telework center, it is equipped with basic office software.

CHOOSING TO ADOPT TELECOMMUTING

23. Consider the following three telecommuting scenarios and answer the questions that follow.

Scenario 1[2]:

Arrangement A	
Minimum:	0 days / week
Maximum:	3 days / week
Schedule:	flexible
Work space:	shared office
Salary:	same
Place:	home
Equipment:	computer, network access
Equipment provider:	employee
Phone bills:	employer
Liability:	employer

Arrangement B	
Minimum:	2 days / week
Maximum:	2 days / week
Schedule:	fixed
Work space:	shared office
Salary:	5% higher
Place:	telework center
Equipment:	computer
Equipment provider:	-------------
Phone bills:	-------------
Liability:	-------------

a. Which arrangement do you prefer?   ( ) A   ( ) B

b. If your preferred arrangement was offered to you, would you telecommute?   ( ) yes   ( ) no

c. How many days per week would you telecommute?   _____ days

d. How would you expect this arrangement to impact your expenditures with:
    child care
    ( ) decrease ___ % ( ) remain the same ( ) increase ___%
    elder care
    ( ) decrease ___ % ( ) remain the same ( ) increase ___%
    home utilities
    ( ) decrease ___ % ( ) remain the same ( ) increase ___%
    overall working costs
    ( ) decrease ___ % ( ) remain the same ( ) increase ___%

---

[2] Three different scenarios were presented to each respondent

e. What type of impact would you expect your preferred arrangement to have on:

	extremely negative							extremely positive	
Your social life	1	2	3	4	5	6	7	8	9
Your family life	1	2	3	4	5	6	7	8	9
Your opportunity for promotion	1	2	3	4	5	6	7	8	9
Your job security	1	2	3	4	5	6	7	8	9
Your schedule flexibility	1	2	3	4	5	6	7	8	9
Your autonomy in your job	1	2	3	4	5	6	7	8	9
Your productivity	1	2	3	4	5	6	7	8	9
The productivity of the group you work with	1	2	3	4	5	6	7	8	9
Your sense of well-being	1	2	3	4	5	6	7	8	9
Your job satisfaction	1	2	3	4	5	6	7	8	9
Your life, overall	1	2	3	4	5	6	7	8	9

24. How would you design your ideal telecommuting arrangement?.

Minimum(days/week):	( ) 0 ( ) 1 ( ) 2 ( ) 3 ( ) 4 ( ) 5
Maximum(days/week):	( ) 1 ( ) 2 ( ) 3 ( ) 4 ( ) 5
Schedule	( ) fixed ( ) flexible
Work space	( ) individual office ( ) shared office ( ) shared desk
Salary	( ) ___% lower ( ) same ( ) ___% higher
Place	( ) home ( ) telework center ( ) either

The following refer to home-based telecommuting only

Equipment	( ) computer ( ) fax ( ) dedicated phone line ( ) network access ( ) other: _____
Equipment provider	( ) employer ( ) employee
Phone bills	( ) employer ( ) employee
Liability	( ) employer ( ) employee

a. If this arrangement was offered to you, would you telecommute?
   ( ) yes   ( ) no

b. How many days per week would you telecommute? _____ days

c. How would you expect this arrangement to impact your expenditures with:

child care
    ( ) decrease ___ % ( ) remain the same ( ) increase ____%
elder care
    ( ) decrease ___ % ( ) remain the same ( ) increase ____%
home utilities
    ( ) decrease ___ % ( ) remain the same ( ) increase ____%
overall working costs
    ( ) decrease ___ % ( ) remain the same ( ) increase ___%
    ( ) increase _____%

d. What type of impact would you expect your telecommuting design to have on:

	extremely negative							extremely positive	
Your social life	1	2	3	4	5	6	7	8	9
Your family life	1	2	3	4	5	6	7	8	9
Your opportunity for promotion	1	2	3	4	5	6	7	8	9
Your job security	1	2	3	4	5	6	7	8	9
Your schedule flexibility	1	2	3	4	5	6	7	8	9
Your autonomy in your job	1	2	3	4	5	6	7	8	9
Your productivity	1	2	3	4	5	6	7	8	9
The productivity of the group you work with	1	2	3	4	5	6	7	8	9
Your sense of well-being	1	2	3	4	5	6	7	8	9
Your job satisfaction	1	2	3	4	5	6	7	8	9
Your life, overall	1	2	3	4	5	6	7	8	9

PERSONAL INFORMATION

25. What industry do you work for?
    ( ) Banking and Finance   ( ) Telecommunication
    ( ) Real Estate   ( ) Computer Software / Hardware
    ( ) Business Services   ( ) Education
    ( ) Government   ( ) Other: _____
    ( ) Consultancy

26. Is the organization you work for currently undergoing any of the following processes?
    ( ) expanding scale   ( ) re engineering
    ( ) reducing scale   ( ) relocating

27. What is your current position?
    ( ) managerial   ( ) sales
    ( ) professional   ( ) other:
    ( ) administrative support, including clerical

28. How long have you been working in your current position? ___ years

29. What is your employment status?
    ( ) full-time salaried   ( ) full-time commissioned
    ( ) part-time salaried   ( ) part-time commissioned
    ( ) hourly paid

30. How long have you been working for this company? ___ years

31. Location of your office   (city and zip code)_____
                      home   (city and zip code)_____

32. What commuting benefits do you receive from your employer?
    ( ) none   ( ) preferred parking
    ( ) mileage expense   ( ) company car
    ( ) transit pass   ( ) other: _____

33. Are you a licensed driver? ( ) yes   ( ) no

34. Do you have an available automobile for your commuting?
    ( ) yes   ( ) no

35. What is your
        gender? ( ) male   ( ) female
        age?_____ years
    marital status? ( ) married   ( ) single   ( ) unmarried

36. If you are married, does your spouse have a paid job?   ( ) yes
        ( ) no

37. What is the highest level of education you have completed?
        ( ) high school   ( ) college   ( ) graduate program

38. What is your annual income before taxes?
        ( ) 19K and under   ( ) 40K to 59K   ( ) 80K to 99K
        ( ) 20K to 39K   ( ) 60K to 79K   ( ) 100K and over

39. What is your household annual income before taxes?
        ( ) 19K and under   ( ) 40K to 59K   ( ) 80K to 99K
        ( ) 20K to 39K   ( ) 60K to 79K   ( ) 100K and over

40. How many persons live in your household in total _____ persons
            children under 6 years of age   _____ children
            children who are currently in day care   _____ children
            elder persons requiring special care   _____ persons

41. Which of the following pieces of equipment or services do you have
    at home (choose as many as apply)?
        ( ) personal computer ( ) more than one phone line
        ( ) fax   ( ) access to a computer network

REFERENCES

[1] L. Bailyn. *Toward the perfect workplace?* Communications of the ACM, Vol.32, No.4, pp.460-471, 1989.

[2] M. Ben-Akiva and S.R. Lerman. *Discrete choice analysis - Theory and application to travel demand.* The MIT Press, Cambridge, Massachusetts, 1985.

[3] A.T. Bernardino, M. Ben-Akiva, and I. Salomon. *A stated preference approach to modeling the adoption of telecommuting.* Transportation Research Record 1413, pp.22-30, 1993.

[4] A.B. Boghani, E.W. Kimble and E.E. Spencer. *Can telecommuting help solve America's transportation problem?* Arthur D. Little, Inc., Acorn Park, Cambridge, MA, 02140, 1991.

[5] K.A. Bollen. *Structural equations with latent variables.* John Wiley & Sons, Inc., New York, NY, 1989.

[6] *The office is a terrible place to work.* Business Week, December 27, 1993.

[7] M. Castell. *The informational city - Information technology, economic restructuring and the urban-regional process.* Blackwell Publishers, Cambridge, MA, 1989

[8] J. Coates, J.Jarrat and J. Mafaffie. *Future work.* The Futurist - May/June, pp.9-19, 1991.

[9] T.B. Cross and M. Raizman. *Telecommuting: the future technology of work.* Dow Jones-Irwin, Homewood, Illinois, 1986.

[10] D.R. Dalton, R.Mesch and J. Debra. *The impact of flexible scheduling on employee attendance.* Administrative Science Quarterly, Vol.35, pp 370-387, 1990.

[11] Department of Commerce, USA. *1990 Census of population and housing*. Bureau of the Census, Data User Services Division, Washington, DC, 20233.

[12] Department of Energy, USA. *Energy, emissions, and social consequences of telecommuting*. Energy efficiency in the US economy. Technical Report One. Washington, DC, 20585, 1994.

[13] Department of Transportation, USA. *Transportation implications of telecommuting*. 1993.

[14] Department of Labor, USA. *Employment and Earnings*. January, 1995,

[15] P. Edwards and S. Edwards. *Working from home - Everything you need to know about living and working under the same roof*. Houghton Mifflin, 1985.

[16] M.E.W. Fritz, K. Higa and S. Narasimham. *Telework: exploring the borderless office*. Proceedings of the Twenty-Seventh Annual Hawaii International Conference on System Sciences, pp.149-158, 1994.

[17] M.B.W. Fritz, K. Higa and S. Narasimham. *Toward a telework taxonomy and test for suitability: a synthesis of the literature*. Group Decision and Negotiation, Forthcoming, 1994.

[18] D.A. Gopinath. *Modeling heterogeneity in discrete choice processes: Application to travel demand* Doctoral dissertation, Department of Civil and Environmental Engineering, Massachusetts Institute of Technology, February, 1995.

[19] G.E. Gordon. *"The dilemmas of telework: technology vs. tradition"*, in Telework: present situation and future development of a new form of work organization. Edited by W.B. Korte, W.J. Steinle and S. Robinson, North-Holland, 1988.

[20] G.E. Gordon and Kelly, *Telecommuting: how to make it work for you and your company*. Prentice-Hall, 1986.

[21] J. Gregory. *Clerical workers and new office technologies*, in <u>Office workstations in the home</u>. National Research Council, Board on Telecommunications and Computer Applications, Commission on Engineering and Technical Systems, National Academy Press, Washington, DC, 1985.

[22] R. Hamer, E. Kroes and H. van Ooststroom. *Teleworking in the Netherlands: an evaluation of changes in travel behaviour*. Transportation, Vol.18, No.4, pp.365-382, 1991.

[23] D.K. Henderson, B.E. Koenig and P.L. Mokhtarian. *Modeling the emissions impact of telecommuting for the Puget Sound Demonstration Project*. Presented at the Transportation Research Board 74th Annual Meeting, Washington, DC, 1995.

[24] J.B. Hopkins, J.O'Donnell and G.T. Ritter. *Telecommuting: how much? how soon?* John A. Volpe National Transportation System Center. US DOT Research and Special Programs Administration, 55 Broadway, Kendall Square, Cambridge, MA 02142, 1994

[25] U. Huws. *New technology and homeworking*. Newsletter of International Labour Studies, April, 1984.

[26] *Conditions of Work Digest*. International Labour Organization, Vol.9, No.1, 1990.

[27] JALA Associates, Inc., *Telecommunications and Energy: the energy conservation implications for California of substitutes for transportation*, California Energy Commission, Sacramento, CA, Report No. p400-83-042, 1983.

[28] R. Kitamura, J.M. Nilles, P. Conroy and D.M. Fleming. *Telecommuting as a transportation planning measure: initial results of State of California Pilot Project*. Transportation Research Record 1285, pp.98-104, 1990.

[29] K.A. Kovack and J.A. Pearce II. *HR strategic mandates for the 1990's*. Personnel, April 1990, pp.50-55.

[30] R.E. Kraut and P. Grambsch. *Prophecy by analogy: potential causes for and consequences of electronic homework.* Bell Communications Research, Morristown, NJ, 1985.

[31] J. Kugelmass. *Telecommuting: a manager's guide to flexible work arrangements.* Lexington Books, New York, NY, 1995.

[32] C.B. Leinberger and C. Lockwood. *How business is reshaping America*, in The Atlantic, pp 43-63, 1986.

[33] LINK Resources Corporation. *1991 Home Office Overview.* No.0322, December, 1991.

[34] H.S. Mahmassani, J.-R. Yen, R. Herman, and M.A. Sullivan. *Employee attitudes and stated preferences towards telecommuting: An exploratory analysis.* Transportation Research Record 1413, pp.31-41, 1993.

[35] P.L. Mokhtarian. *Telecommuting and travel: state of the practice, state of the art.* Transportation - Vol.18, No.4, pp.319-342, 1991.

[36] P.L. Mokhtarian and I. Salomon. *Modeling the choice of telecommuting: setting the context.* Environment and Planning A 26(5), pp.749-766, 1994.

[37] P.L. Mokhtarian and I. Salomon. *Modeling the choice of telecommuting 2: a case of the preferred impossible alternative.* Submitted to Environment and Planning A, 1994.

[38] P.L. Mokhtarian and I. Salomon. *Modeling the desire to telecommute: the importance of attitudinal factors in behavioral models.* Submitted to Transportation Research B, 1994.

[39] P.L. Mokhtarian and I. Salomon. *Modeling the choice of telecommuting 3: identifying the choice set and estimating binary choice models for technology-based alternatives.* Submitted to Environment and Planning A, 1995.

[40] J.M. Nilles. *Traffic reduction by telecommuting: A status review and selected bibliography.* Transportation Research A - Vol.22A, No.4, pp.301- 317, 1989.

[41] J.M. Nilles. *Telecommuting and urban sprawl: mitigator or inciter?* Transportation, Vol.18, No.4, pp.365-382, 1991.

[42] M.H.Olson. *New information technology and organization culture.* Management Information System Quartely - Vol.6, No.5, pp.71-92, 1982.

[43] M.H. Olson. *Work at home for computer professionals: Current attitudes and future prospects.* ACM Transactions on Office Information Systems - Vol.7, No.4, pp.317-338, 1989.

[44] M.H. Olson and S.B. Primps. *Working at home with computers: work and nonwork issues.* Journal of Social Issues, Vol.40, No.3, pp.97-112, 1984.

[45] J.H. Pratt. *Characteristics of Telecommuters.* Presented at the Transportation Research Board 73rd Annual Meeting, January 9-13, 1994, Washington, DC.

[46] R.M. Pendyala, K.G. Goulias and R. Kitamura. *Impact of telecommuting on spatial and temporal patterns of household travel.* Transportation, Vol.18, No.4, pp.383-410, 1991.

[47] W.L. Renfro. *Second thoughts on moving the office home*, in Information Technology Revolution. Edited by T. Forester, Basil Blackwell, 1985.

[48] I. Salomon. *Telecommunications and travel relationships: a review.* Transportation Research A, Vol.20A, No.3, pp.223-238, 1986.

[49] S. Sampath, S. Saxena and P.L. Mokhtarian. *The effectiveness of telecommuting as a transportation control measure.* Proceedings of the ASCE Urban Transportation Division National Conference on Transportation Planning and Air Quality. Santa Barbara, CA, pp.347-362, 1991.

[50] W.A. Spinks. *Satellite and resort offices in Japan.* Transportation, Vol.18, No.4, pp.343-363, 1991.

[51] M.A. Sullivan., H.S. Mahmassani, and J.-R. Yen. *A choice model of employee participation in telecommuting under a cost-neutral scenario.* Transportation Research Record 1413, pp.31-41, 1993.

[52] J.-R. Yen, H.S. Mahmassani, R. Herman. *Employer attitude and stated preferences towards telecommuting: an exploratory analysis.* Presented at the Transportation Research Board 73rd Annual Meeting, January 9-13, 1994, Washington, DC.

Index

For Product Safety Concerns and Information please contact our EU
representative GPSR@taylorandfrancis.com Taylor & Francis Verlag GmbH,
Kaufingerstraße 24, 80331 München, Germany

Printed and bound by CPI Group (UK) Ltd, Croydon, CR0 4YY
08/05/2025
01864426-0003